GUIDI

September–December 2024

Edited by **Rachel Tranter** and **Olivia Warburton**

BRF Ministries

15 The Chambers, Vineyard
Abingdon OX14 3FE
brf.org.uk

Bible Reading Fellowship is a charity (233280)
and company limited by guarantee (301324),
registered in England and Wales

ISBN 978 1 80039 265 6

Distributed in Australia by:
MediaCom Education Inc, PO Box 610, Unley, SA 5061
Tel: 1 800 811 311 | admin@mediacom.org.au

Distributed in New Zealand by:
Scripture Union Wholesale, PO Box 760, Wellington
Tel: 04 385 0421 | suwholesale@clear.net.nz

Acknowledgements

Scripture quotations marked with the following abbreviations are taken from the
version shown. Where no abbreviation is given, the quotation is taken from the
version stated in the contributor's introduction.

NASB: the New American Standard Bible®, Copyright © 1960, 1962, 1963, 1968,
1971, 1972, 1973, 1975, 1977, 1995 by The Lockman Foundation. Used by
permission. (**www.Lockman.org**). NRSV: the New Revised Standard Version
Updated Edition. Copyright © 2021 National Council of Churches of Christ in the
United States of America. Used by permission. All rights reserved worldwide. NIV:
the Holy Bible, New International Version (Anglicised edition) copyright © 1979,
1984, 2011 by Biblica. Used by permission of Hodder & Stoughton Publishers, a
Hachette UK company. All rights reserved. 'NIV' is a registered trademark of Biblica.
UK trademark number 1448790. ESV: the Holy Bible, English Standard Version,
published by HarperCollins Publishers, © 2001 Crossway Bibles, a division of Good
News Publishers. Used by permission. All rights reserved. RSV: Revised Standard
Version of the Bible, copyright © 1946, 1952, and 1971 the Division of Christian
Education of the National Council of the Churches of Christ in the United States of
America. Used by permission. All rights reserved.

Every effort has been made to trace and contact copyright owners for material used
in this resource. We apologise for any inadvertent omissions or errors, and would
ask those concerned to contact us so that full acknowledgement can be made in
the future.

A catalogue record for this book is available from the British Library

Printed and bound in the UK by Zenith Media NP4 0DQ

Suggestions for using *Guidelines*

Set aside a regular time and place, if possible, when and where you can read and pray undisturbed. Before you begin, take time to be still and, if you find it helpful, use the BRF Ministries prayer on page 6.

In *Guidelines*, the introductory section provides context for the passages or themes to be studied, while the units of comment can be used daily, weekly or whatever best fits your timetable. You will need a Bible (more than one if you want to compare different translations) as Bible passages are not included. Please don't be tempted to skip the Bible reading because you know the passage well. We will have utterly failed if we don't bring our readers into engagement with the word of God. At the end of each week is a 'Guidelines' section, offering further thoughts about, or practical application of, what you have been studying.

Occasionally, you may read something in *Guidelines* that you find particularly challenging, even uncomfortable. This is inevitable in a series of notes which draws on a wide spectrum of contributors and doesn't believe in ducking difficult issues. Indeed, we believe that *Guidelines* readers much prefer thought-provoking material to a bland diet that only confirms what they already think.

If you do disagree with a contributor, you may find it helpful to go through these three steps. First, think about why you feel uncomfortable. Perhaps this is an idea that is new to you, or you are not happy about the way something has been expressed. Or there may be something more substantial – you may feel that the writer is guilty of sweeping generalisation, factual error, or theological or ethical misjudgement. Second, pray that God would use this disagreement to teach you more about his word and about yourself. Third, have a deeper read about the issue. There are further reading suggestions at the end of each writer's block of notes. And then, do feel free to write to the contributor or the editor of *Guidelines*. We welcome communication, by email, phone or letter, as it enables us to discover what has been useful, challenging or infuriating for our readers. We don't always promise to change things, but we will always listen and think about your ideas, complaints or suggestions. Thank you!

To send feedback, please email **enquiries@brf.org.uk**, phone **+44 (0)1865 319700** or write to the address shown opposite.

Writers in this issue

Isabelle Hamley is principal of Ridley Hall. She has previously held posts as a theological adviser to the Church of England's House of Bishops, parish priest, tutor in Old Testament and chaplain to the Archbishop of Canterbury.

George Wieland is a research fellow at Carey Baptist College, New Zealand, where he formerly taught New Testament and mission. He and his wife Jo pastored in Brazil and the UK before moving to New Zealand.

Leoné Martin is an associate pastor at Cannon Street Memorial Baptist Church. She is completing a theology research masters at Bristol Baptist College.

Bill Goodman encourages and enables lifelong learning among clergy and other church leaders in the Anglican diocese of Sheffield, UK. *Yearning for You* is the published version of his Sheffield PhD.

Helen Paynter is a Baptist minister, and teaches biblical studies at Bristol Baptist College. She is also the founding director of the Centre for the Study of Bible and Violence (**csbvbristol.org.uk**).

Max Kramer is chaplain of Keble College, Oxford. His academic interests include classics, biblical studies and Hellenistic Judaism. He is also author of *The Canterbury Book of New Parish Prayers* (Canterbury Press, 2021).

Andrew Boakye is lecturer in religions and theology at the University of Manchester and co-chair of the Paul Seminar of the British New Testament Society. He is the author of *Death and Life* (Pickwick, 2017), a book about Galatians.

Olivia Warburton is co-editor of *Guidelines*. Most recently head of content creation and Living Faith ministry lead for BRF Ministries, she has worked in a number of editorial roles.

David Spriggs has been a Baptist minister for over 50 years, serving in six different churches. For 20 of those years he worked for the Evangelical Alliance and Bible Society. He has three married children and ten grandchildren.

Rachel Tranter is content creation team lead at BRF Ministries, as well as being co-editor of *Guidelines*. She has a certificate in mission from Cliff College.

Elizabeth Dodd is a lecturer at Sarum College and research associate for the Oxford Centre for Religion and Culture. She writes on poetry and theology, particularly the lyric forms of praise and prayer.

Cally Hammond is dean of Gonville and Caius College, Cambridge, where she teaches New Testament Greek and early Christian history. She is the author of *Augustine's Life of Prayer, Learning and Love* (BRF, 2019).

The editors write…

This issue of *Guidelines* has been designed to guide and nourish you. We hope that you will enjoy it, and thank you, as ever, for the feedback you've provided on previous issues.

Bill Goodman reaches the end of his epic series on the book of Psalms in this issue. Andrew Boakye also concludes his series on Galatians, taking us from chapter 3 to the end of the book. Isabelle Hamley takes up the mantle for our gospel series, guiding us on 'a journey in discipleship' as we look at Luke 9—16.

Our Old Testament series for this issue are Esther, written by former *Guidelines* editor Helen Payner, and Joshua, written by Leoné Martin. Neither make particularly comfortable reading, but our hope is that both provide you with a deeper understanding of who God is.

In the New Testament, George Wieland helps us with the short books of Titus and Philemon. Olivia Warburton takes us on a whistle-stop tour of New Testament prayers, whetting our appetite for delving deeper into this topic ourselves. Max Kramer helps us to think through the politics of Jesus, and what this means for ourselves as Christians formulating our own political views.

As we journey into Advent, we are in good company. David Spriggs invites us to think about forgiveness, while Elizabeth Dodd invites us to ponder the poetry of the Magnificat: a song of victory, a prophetic poem and a hymn of praise. Meanwhile, Rachel Tranter looks at the use of the Old Testament in the New Testament, with examples from Matthew, Ephesians and Revelation. These different types of uses help us to contextualise the Old Testament and understand how the New Testament writers saw the scriptures in light of Jesus' life, death and resurrection. Finally, Cally Hammond reflects on how, where and when we find Jesus in the world.

As we journey through the final section of the year towards our Advent celebrations, we hope that these notes continue to draw you closer to the love of God expressed through Jesus.

Rachel   *Olivia*

The prayer of BRF Ministries

Faithful God,
thank you for growing BRF
from small beginnings
into the worldwide family of BRF Ministries.
We rejoice as young and old
discover you through your word
and grow daily in faith and love.
Keep us humble in your service,
ambitious for your glory
and open to new opportunities.
For your name's sake.
Amen.

Helping to pay it forward

As part of our Living Faith ministry, we're raising funds to give away copies of Bible reading notes and other resources to those who aren't able to access them any other way, working with food banks and chaplaincy services, in prisons, hospitals and care homes.

'This very generous gift will be hugely appreciated, and truly bless each recipient… Bless you for your kindness.'

'We would like to send our enormous thanks to all involved. Your generosity will have a significant impact and will help us to continue to provide support to local people in crisis, and for this we cannot thank you enough.'

If you've enjoyed and benefited from our resources, would you consider paying it forward to enable others to do so too?

Make a gift at **brf.org.uk/donate**

'Lord, teach us': a journey in discipleship through Luke 9—16

Isabelle Hamley

The phrase 'Lord, teach us' encapsulates the middle section of the gospel of Luke. Jesus teaches through word and example, through story and short, pithy sayings, through healings and deliverance, in inviting the disciples to join him and sending them out themselves. As he does so, a picture of discipleship and of the shape of the community that Jesus is gathering gradually emerges. It is a community shaped by the values of the kingdom of God – radical alternative ways of thinking, behaving and relating that nurture the flourishing of all at the expense of none. Jesus' teaching is challenging: there is much talk of judgement and of the cost of following him. Discipleship is costly, but the alternative is worse over the long run.

Perhaps the most salient aspect of Jesus' teaching in these eight chapters is the sheer volume of sayings and stories about wealth, and its associated status and power. Wealth is not condemned as intrinsically wrong, though it can be wrongly acquired. However, wealth that is not used for the welfare of all, wealth that does not lead to the blessing of the entire community, can be a burden and a curse to the one who holds it. Similarly, those with status and power are called, again and again, to use it for the benefit of all, whether this is exercised in an economic, political or religious sphere. Jesus is clearly concerned, not just with individuals, but with communities, their lives together and the way in which our daily choices shape the health and flourishing of those around us.

Unless otherwise stated, Bible quotations are taken from the NRSV.

1 From guests to hosts

Luke 9:1–17

Luke loves collapsing paradoxes, challenging embedded ways of thinking which prevent the gospel from taking root among the people of God. Early in chapter 9, Jesus is preparing disciples to become leaders among the people of God and sends out the twelve. We need to read the stories of the sending out and the feeding of the five thousand together if we want to get the gist of what Jesus is teaching future leaders of the church and all disciples.

The twelve are sent out with power – over all demons and to cure diseases. Yet at the same time, they are told to take nothing with them, and 'nothing' is emphasised by being placed right at the beginning of Jesus' instructions in Greek. Alongside immense power, the disciples are placed in a position of immense vulnerability, utterly dependent on the kindness of strangers. Mission is set up right from the start as a cooperative enterprise, where 'missionaries' are guests among others. This inevitably shapes how the gospel is preached and healing offered. Power dynamics are evened out, mutual respect and care required. Mission includes both proclamation and healing/deliverance. The gospel is for the whole person. Bodies matter in the landscape of the kingdom of God, and Jesus gives no mandate for separating a spiritual gospel from a social gospel. The gospel call is all-encompassing; it demands that we engage the whole person and collapse, rather than build, any divide between the sacred and the secular, between what belongs to spirituality and what does not. Everything is affected by the gospel.

And then… Jesus turns the tables. Those who were guests now become co-hosts with him as he feeds the crowd. Jesus again models holding teaching and feeding together, caring for bodies and souls together. From the scarcity of the disciples' sending out with 'nothing', we move to the sheer overabundance of the kingdom and twelve baskets of leftovers. The disciples, who had gone out to teach, a traditional male role with status, now serve food, a role usually reserved for women and slaves.

Leaders and disciples of Jesus are called to an integrity of life that does not seek status or raw power, but holds out the gospel as gift, models vulnerability and serves the people through teaching and service, by being guests as much as being hosts.

2 He is not who you think he is

'Who do you say that I am?' is one of the most famous questions of the gospel. Who is this Jesus? Jesus probes the disciples' understanding and does not let them rely on hearsay and the words of others. He first asks, what do the crowds say? But this is not enough. Knowing *of* Jesus is not the same as knowing Jesus. Rumours of God are not the same as encounter with God. Yet Jesus takes the disciples further. How do we discern who Jesus is, and where Jesus is at work? This is a crucial question for those of us reading at a distance. We no longer have the benefit of walking with Jesus physically, daily. We are dependent on the testimony of others, and on other disciples teaching us to recognise Jesus around us and at work in our own lives.

This passage helps by telling us that Jesus is rarely where and who we want him to be. Yes, Jesus is the Jesus of the transfiguration, on a mountain, shining brightly. This Jesus may be easy to recognise – or is he? It is not a coincidence that Jesus' teaching on suffering comes before the transfiguration. It is easy to look for God on the mountaintops, in exciting places, in amazing experiences that transcend everything we know. These experiences are few and far between, and they carry danger with them: the danger of thinking that God is in the shiny, amazing places of the world, that God is found in places of power and glory, and that it is through these experiences that we meet with God.

The drift of this passage is the exact opposite. The Messiah 'must undergo great suffering', 'be rejected' and 'killed' (v. 22) before he is finally 'raised'. The danger is that we look for the resurrection without going through the cross, aim for glory without vulnerability, power without weakness. Instead, Jesus teaches that the way to God is found through the cross first, in unexpected places and in unexpected ways. Just as with the birth narratives, Jesus' presence is often hidden in places we overlook, because we look for glory and palaces rather than humility in small towns and crowded family rooms, as in Bethlehem. Jesus will often be found at work in these modest places, and we recognise Jesus' followers, not by their glory, but the fact that they, too, 'take up their cross', and follow him.

3 Did you really listen?

Luke 9:46–62

When the disciples were sent out at the beginning of chapter 9, they were given enormous power – and taught that this power needed exercising alongside the vulnerability and humility of taking 'nothing' with them, and depending on the generosity of others. Jesus then teaches them about the cost of discipleship. Did they really listen? Did they simply not understand?

Here, only a little later, we find the disciples preoccupied with power and glory, more than ready to misuse the immense responsibility entrusted them. They fight over who is the greatest, as if they had not been taught to serve at tables like the least. They want to stop someone else casting out demons in the name of Jesus, as if power granted to others threatens their own, and forgetting that deliverance is characteristic of God's own work. They seem to think that the gospel is their private property. When they go through a Samaritan village and are not welcome, they want to use the power of God not for healing, deliverance or proclamation, but only to destroy, rather than simply 'shake the dust off their feet' as they had been commanded (9:5).

Learning how to use power well is difficult, and learning that God is not found primarily in great displays of power is even harder. Jesus has to remind them again, and again, and again.

The disciples struggle to put Jesus, rather than themselves, at the centre. By putting Jesus at the centre, their gaze would actually be directed outward, towards the healing and deliverance of the world around them. Putting Jesus at the centre would also achieve something quite different in terms of relationships between the disciples. In the first subsection (vv. 46–48), they compete with one another, rather than seeking to serve and work together. In the second subsection (vv. 49–50), they seek to undermine the work of someone who also follows Jesus, thereby bringing fragmentation and competition between different groups of disciples. Bringing disunity within the body, treating other believers as if they do not really belong because they operate slightly differently, is something that will occupy much of the letters of Paul. Human tribes and factions here get in the way of the gospel, and Jesus firmly stands against them, and returns to teaching about how to follow him truly (vv. 57–62).

4 Expanding the imagination

Luke 10:1–24

Here, Luke tells a story remarkably similar to the one that opened chapter 9: the sending out of the 72, with instructions similar to those given to the twelve, but expanded. The progress of the narrative through Luke and Acts shows how ever-widening circles of disciples are brought into the proclamation of the kingdom of God. The story is darker here than in chapter 9. Following the disciples' struggles to understand the message, and rejection in Samaria, the themes of rejection and judgement take on more prominence. The challenge of the gospel and the cost of discipleship become embodied in the reality of conflict.

In today's world, churches in decline often try to make the gospel more attractive or see rejection as a sign of failure on their part. This passage in Luke, however, reminds us that rejection was the experience of Jesus and of early disciples, because the gospel is good news, but it is not easy. The demands of the gospel are obvious in the instructions to the 72. They are to go out with no purse, no bag and no sandals (v. 4). In other words, no containers for worldly goods, and no sign of wealth. It is an instruction to operate outside of economic norms of service and payment, and outside of the norms of sensible, prudent provision ahead of journeys. It is a call back to the desert in Exodus, when Israel was led by God into a place of utter scarcity and asked to trust in God's provision. This kind of instruction demands a radical shift of the imagination, the ability to imagine that different ways to live and to relate are possible. It demands trust, and the belief that human life and survival are essentially relational, rather than based on individual planning and provision-making. Obliquely, it is a challenge to the economic thinking of the Roman Empire, and every other system that has sought the accumulation of riches as a marker of success.

Jesus proclaims that the kingdom of God is ruled by different principles – abundance, faith, trust and generosity – which are neither naïve, nor a pipe dream. But this is hard teaching, and the disciples are not always welcome.

And yet, whether they are met with peace and welcome, or rejection, the message, and the invitation, are the same: the kingdom of God is near.

5 Who is my neighbour?

Luke 10:25–42

The good Samaritan is perhaps the best-known of all of Jesus' parables. The term has made it into everyday language. Familiarity can mean we miss its shock value, and its more subtle challenges. We know about the animosity between Jews and Samaritans, a rivalry that clearly went both ways. Here, the story challenges the caricaturing of the 'other' – and of the self.

This is not a new theme. The Old Testament tells of times when Israel thinks that Israelites are the only safe people to be with, while denigrating the inhabitants of the land (e.g. Judges 19). The assumption is then often proved wrong with Israelite turning against Israelite. One of the subtexts of these stories, and of this parable, is that belonging to a group does not guarantee that the group will care for you. And simply belonging to an 'other' group does not guarantee that a person will behave according to our worst predictions. The story challenges the building of prejudice and discrimination based on nothing more than identity; it also challenges the idea that 'my group' is necessarily better or holier. It is a good parable for the digital age of echo chambers and culture wars.

Jesus challenges his listeners to expand their imagination, unlearn destructive ways shaped by culture and daily life, and trust that things could be different. Here, he challenges the instinct to fear the stranger. Again, this is not new. The Old Testament commands repeatedly to care for 'the widow, the orphan and the stranger' (Deuteronomy 10:18), and to 'love [our] neighbour' (Leviticus 19:18). Love is easy when it is only a concept, when it is not tied to fear, a sense of threat, uncertainty, or to risk and loss for ourselves. By telling this story, Jesus puts flesh on the bones of the command to love, and shows its cost – and its reward. We often imagine ourselves as the Samaritan in the story, told to go and love, but the audience was Jewish: the person they are invited to identify with is not first the Samaritan, but the injured man. The Jewish man is hurt, and loved by his neighbour – the fearsome, strange, despised Samaritan. The parable suggests that loving our neighbour is a two-way street, where our capacity to love can only grow as we accept the gift of the stranger.

6 Teach us to pray

In Luke's sequence of teaching on discipleship, it is logical to incorporate a section on how to pray. The disciples' question is interesting – 'teach us to pray, as John taught his disciples'. What were they thinking? Are there right and wrong ways to pray? Would John have taught a different technique? There is a fine line between being open to teaching, exploring and expanding spirituality, and thinking that there is a failsafe trick to our spiritual disciplines, that if we do it the right way, it works. Jesus gives three sets of teaching on prayer. Together, they remind us that prayer is not a formula but, first and foremost, about who we pray to: God, who loves us as a parent loves a child, and who will only give us good things.

Jesus' form of words is instructive. Instead of going for something different, it digs deep into the stories and practices of Israel. God is 'our father' in the same way that Israel is God's child in the Old Testament – it is a collective identity which speaks of love and closeness, and of a call to live as God does. Yet in the same breath as God is an intimate and close parent, he is also 'in heaven' and 'hallowed'. The hallowing of God's name sets a distance between humans and God, and reminds us that God is immeasurably greater than we are, in power and holiness. Holding together closeness and distance, intimacy and reverence, is the challenge here, one that reflects a paradox expressed in the words of Isaiah (e.g. 40:10–11) or Hosea (e.g. 6:1). God is also king, as God is king throughout the Old Testament, despite human kings who often try and usurp God's true kingship.

The daily bread line harks back to manna in the desert and God's command to only take enough for the day ahead and not hoard for tomorrow bread that belongs to another's today. Forgiveness directs our eyes to the One who forgives – the God who, in the Old Testament, is characterised as 'a God merciful and gracious, slow to anger, and abounding in steadfast love and faithfulness… forgiving iniquity and transgression and sin' (Exodus 34:6–7).

Jesus' teaching on prayer, first and foremost, directs the disciple towards God and his faithfulness throughout Israel's history.

Guidelines

Jesus is shaping a people as he travels with the disciples, teaches the crowds and comes into conversation with religious and secular leaders. His questions and teaching constantly challenge the disciples to ask – did you really listen? Do you really understand what this means? How far does Jesus' teaching really penetrate our thought patterns, our habits and our character?

Are we willing to be guests and hosts, to share our wealth and offer hospitality? And are we willing to make ourselves vulnerable as guests in others' homes – in workplaces, in secular institutions, with those of other faiths, sharing the gospel and peace graciously and respectfully, and accepting what the other has to offer and teach us?

Jesus' most salient challenge is, perhaps, the less obvious one: the challenge to let our imaginations be transformed by a picture of the kingdom that is so alien, so different from our ways of living and structuring our communities, that it completely disrupts our expectations about relationships, money and possessions and the degree to which we trust God for all we need.

9–15 September

1 Deliverance

Luke 11:14–32

After teaching on prayer, Jesus moves to teaching on deliverance – a logical link given that the final line of the Lord's Prayer is 'deliver us from evil'. But there is a big gap for the watching crowds between a line in a prayer and a live miracle from Jesus.

Jesus starts with practical action. Casting out demons has already been marked out in chapters 9 and 10 as a sign of God's kingdom breaking into the world. Deliverance, which releases people into fullness of life, in relation to God and to community, is one of the good gifts of God that is available through prayer. Yet the crowds do not immediately recognise this as a gift, and they divide into two.

Some doubt that this is the work of God, and attribute 'deliverance', an action typical of God throughout scripture (though in the Old Testament, it is deliverance from enemies, but never demons), to Beelzebul, a symbol of evil. This section of the crowd, as Jesus then unpacks, mixes up their understanding of good and evil, and fails to recognise God at work, or a prophet, by their fruit.

Another section of the crowd asks for a sign from heaven. One might want to say, how much more of a sign do you need than a full healing! Asking for signs and testing God is what the devil does earlier in the gospel, when Jesus is taken to the desert to be tempted. Yet here, the crowds are doing the testing and demanding a sign, instead of praying, as they have been told, 'do not bring us to the day of trial/testing/temptation, but deliver us from evil' (11:4, my translation).

The crowd watches the miracle like a show, and comments on it, failing to realise that they themselves are caught up in the spiritual battle it exemplifies. Jesus brings them in by telling them, 'whoever is not with me is against me' (v. 23). Deliverance, miracles, answers to prayer, are not a spectacle or a story 'out there' for us to judge, evaluate, approve or condemn. They are symptoms of a reality we are all caught up in, which begs listeners then, and readers now, to decide which master to follow.

2 Woe to you

Luke 11:33–54

The narrative takes a darker turn at the end of chapter 11, with conflict between Jesus and Jewish authorities growing more entrenched. It is important to understand the type of exchange between the different parties at the Pharisees' house. There was a culture of relating between different schools of philosophies in the ancient world that was marked by mutual slander and accusations, seen between Greek philosophers (Stoics and Epicureans, for instance, but also between Jewish parties). This doesn't take away the weight of Jesus' criticism, but it tempers the dialogue and avoids overstating Jesus' lack of tact as a guest. Jesus is also acting as a prophet: he teaches through both words and actions (deliberately failing to wash: he washes on other occasions, so here, he is making a point).

Jesus's teaching moves away from disciples as a whole to concentrate on leaders in general, and religious leaders in particular. The task of leadership is primarily one of service, enabling the people to grow closer to God and live lives that exemplify the values and practices of the kingdom. He accuses leaders of seeking their own good rather than the good of the whole people, of loving the status and privileges that leadership confers rather than leading with humility and generosity, of suppressing truth and truth-tellers, and of hoarding knowledge that should be shared so that others can flourish. Leaders behaving like this are guilty of injustice, and dereliction of duty. Leadership exists solely to enable the flourishing of all.

Jesus' accusations stand as a warning to all leaders, in any sphere, at any time. The temptations of power, of hoarding riches, and of using one's position to set oneself above others is one that many have fallen into – in the church, in industry, in politics. Ultimately, the question that faces leaders is, are you still being disciples? Are you still striving to follow God and model your life according to the ways of God? If so, then justice, service and love of others will guide the shape of leadership, as it should guide the actions of every disciple in all walks of life.

3 On the day of trial

Luke 12:1–12

'Do not bring us to the time of trial…' was the prayer of Luke 11. Yet here, in chapter 12, Jesus addresses squarely days of trial, when the temptation to turn away from the gospel and go the easy way may arise. This follows logically from the attack on Jesus and determination of a small group to catch him out (11:53–54). Jesus has consistently called his disciples to follow him and imitate him. If he is put at risk in his prophetic ministry, his followers, who share the same life and proclaim the same gospel, will be at risk too.

Prayer sometimes goes unanswered, and the day of trial comes. If it does, then Jesus makes a series of promises for those who will face it: whatever is done to them and their bodies, they, as persons, still have integrity, worth and dignity that cannot be taken away, because God cares for them and will see them through. It is not that bodies do not matter, but that their personhood, their worth, cannot be taken away. Their life is 'hidden with Christ in God' (Colossians 3:3).

Before the encouragement, however, Jesus speaks of the need for transparency, warning that nothing remains secret forever. Secrets have a habit of leaking out, and basing one's life on secrets, rather than trusting in God's mercy, is a waste of time and a rather significant mistake. Jesus' teaching here is particularly appropriate for a digital age, where many say and type all kinds of things online, that will never be fully erased, and often come back to haunt them many years later. This is not to diminish or dismiss the need for privacy; but privacy and secrecy are two very different concepts. Privacy is about the protection of someone's dignity and personhood, and appropriate respect for the boundaries between self and other. Secrecy misuses privacy to hide what is detrimental to others and shield the self from responsibility and accountability. Discerning where appropriate privacy stops and damaging secrecy begins is an essential task of discipleship.

4 Rich fools and wise birds

Luke 12:13–21

Jesus said more about money than he did about prayer or sex – even though the fact is not always obvious in our lives or our churches. Here, he again offers some hard teaching, tempered by a wider assurance of God's loving care.

A man comes and asks for his help. The man's cry is a cry for justice. In all likelihood, his father had died without a will. Under these circumstances, the younger brother would be left landless unless the older brother agreed the property could be divided up. Why doesn't Jesus help? Jesus' answer, 'who set me to be a judge over you?' shows that Jesus refuses to be drawn into a family quarrel and risk undermining the relationship further. His authority would be unlikely to be recognised by the older brother, and any pronouncement would deepen the rift. Jesus does not know the whole story, or all involved. Justice cannot be completely one-sided; nor can it properly happen independently of the mending of relationships.

The parable Jesus tells next continues the theme, albeit obliquely. The rich man of the story is a man who is constantly seeking for more and places his trust and security in material possessions. He is not blamed for being prudent but for over-relying on material things, and for satisfying his need for security without thinking of the needs of others. He is an example for the two brothers of life without justice – for those who think that material possessions are everything and they must gather them, and for those who gather for themselves with no thought for who they may wrong, ignore or fail to notice in the process. The rich man's fate is tragic, and not simply for his premature death. In verses 17–18, we are privy to his deliberations of what to do with his wealth. He deliberates alone: no family, no friends, no community, to share either the burden of decision-making or the surplus of his abundance. Ultimately, the man is alone, and his possessions amount to nothing. When he meets God, he has had no more relationship with God than with others around him. Wealth has isolated him, and made him less, rather than more, secure in the world.

5 From master to servant

Luke 12:35–59

Jesus' next parable (35–38) revisits a theme explored in chapter 9, where Jesus, and the disciples, moved fluidly between being guest and host, powerful and vulnerable. Here, the distinction between master and servants is collapsed and redrawn. The parable opens with the injunction that servants should make themselves ready by dressing for action. People in ancient Palestine wore loose, long robes, ideally suited to hot weather. This kind of vestment wasn't ideal for physically demanding work, whether walking on dusty roads or working in domestic settings. Preparing oneself therefore meant using a belt to gather the robe and lift it off the floor so it wouldn't get dirty, or in the way. The servants are not simply told to stay awake, ready to open the door. They are told to be prepared for serious hard work, ready for any eventuality. As a metaphor for discipleship, it suggests that the whole person needs to be serving God, and everything ready to respond to the call of the gospel. It is hard teaching again.

Today we baulk at the language of slavery, quite rightly, and at the idea that anyone can be required to give everything to a master. But the master of the parable is no usual master. He leaves the wedding feast and comes back. There may be tension, and worry: is the master trying to catch the servants out? Why is he coming home alone? And why knock on the door of his own house?

When the master comes, the tables are turned unexpectedly. For those servants who welcome him home, the master becomes servant. He himself dresses for hard labour (in the same words used in verse 35), and he himself serves them (v. 37). They are invited to recline at the table, and he will serve. The servants no longer need their belts and working attire; they no longer have their entire being directed towards another. Instead, the master himself serves them, cares for them and takes on the clothes of humility and hard work.

The synoptic gospels do not have an account of the washing of feet at the last supper, but this parable, in effect, has the same underlying message: this is your God, whom you serve, and who serves you. Be ready to serve, as he does.

6 All that oppresses

The pattern we are now familiar with occurs here again: Jesus starts with a stark and sombre story, and follows it with one that affirms God's care. Here, he starts with two news stories that have got people talking, one of a random accident, the other a result of Pilate's evil (which, incidentally, foreshadows Jesus' own death as a Galilean before Pilate). Jesus decisively dismisses any link between suffering and sin. It is always tempting, when faced with suffering, to try and explain it. If we can explain these people's death through their sin, then it means there is something we can do to avoid their fate. Accepting there is no link brings us into a world that is more random, less controllable and scarier.

Within this world, Jesus encourages the disciples to focus, not on the sins of others, and not on what they can't control, but on what is their personal responsibility – their own life of faith. His words are initially terse: 'unless you repent you will all perish just as they did' (v. 3). Jesus does not mean that those who repent will never die; but rather that repentance makes a difference to how we die – and live. His words are softened with the story of the fig tree. A tree that does not yield fruit is useless – but this tree is given a reprieve. In the economy of God, there is space for grace and second chances.

These first two sections frame what happens next, with a healing on the sabbath. In a world trying to explain evil and suffering, it would have been easy to condemn the woman as bearing her own evil. But Jesus' teaching undermines this, as do his words, calling her a daughter of Abraham, and her actions, praising God. There are many things that burden and oppress in the world, and those are often talked about as 'spirits' in the gospel, with little detail. The point of the narrative is not to apportion blame, as with the tower and Pilate, but to focus on the possibility of deliverance and redemption. Focusing on deliverance and the action of God is what the local religious leaders forgot, and, in the process, they forgot to see a woman, her suffering and the amazing possibilities of the kingdom.

Guidelines

Jesus' teaching touches on multiple areas of discipleship, with a warning that discipleship needs to go deep and transform the whole person. Jesus' warnings to Pharisees and scribes are not ones we can sweep aside; instead, they beg all disciples to consider how they practise justice, how they care for their character and not just what is seen from the outside, and how they handle power, status and possessions, and their temptations, in whatever form they may arise. How do you nurture your own discipleship in different areas of your life? Who walks with you on the road of discipleship, to encourage, accompany and help you be honest with yourself? Whose voice of challenge are you willing to listen to?

Honesty is one aspect of discipleship that Jesus particularly homes in on, with teaching about secrecy. You may want to ponder how privacy and secrecy work in your own life and place of work. Are these boundaries respected? Is there any unhelpful secrecy that needs challenging?

16–22 September

1 Mustard and flour

Luke 13:18–35

These two short parables, the mustard seed and the woman baking, are both domestic parables, hinting at daily life. Mustard was both a condiment and a medicinal herb. As such, it refers to two aspects of the kingdom: the abundance of food, banquets, feeding, on the one hand, and healing on the other. Mustard was used to draw poison out of snake bites, to help with digestive ailments, to relieve pain and soothe congestion in poultices. Jesus picked his illustration appropriately, and pairs it with the consistent overabundance of the kingdom. Just like the feeding of the 5,000, where a few loaves and fishes feed a crowd, here a small seed which normally never turns into more than a bush becomes a tree big enough for birds. This image of the kingdom is one that encompasses the whole of creation. Jesus often uses pictures from the natural world; it is easy to over-spiritualise these. However, in the logic of scripture, human beings are an integral part of creation, rooted in the soil used to create them (Genesis 2), and their actions affect not just people but the land itself. It is the whole of creation that 'waits with eager longing' for God's action (Romans 8:19), and the whole cosmos, all things created, visible and invisible, will be reconciled to God in Christ, the firstborn of all *creation* (Colossians 1:15–20).

The second parable moves into the domain of a woman baking bread. The amount of bread she is baking is far more than one family would need, but likely will feed several households. Women often joined together to grind, knead and bake. There is a relational, communal element to this picture of the kingdom, a sense of giving away the fruit of one's labour for the flourishing of the community. The 'three measures of flour' are not a random choice. It is the amount of flour that Sarah baked for the three angelic visitors of Genesis 18:6; it is also what Hannah offered when her precious baby, Samuel, an answer to prayer, was presented in the temple (1 Samuel 1:24). There is a hint here that the coming of the kingdom is about the revelation of God. This revelation is rarely obvious in Luke, and the woman's action could be translated as 'hides' (rather than 'mixes') the yeast. God's action is visible to those who know the signs and are alert, yet hidden for many.

2 Table manners and table matters

Luke 14:1–24

Meals matter in the gospel. Jesus is often found teaching around mealtimes, and one of his most famous miracles is feeding the crowds. We need to read the parables of banquets in this chapter together with the prophetic sign of the feeding of the 5,000. The overall pattern of Jesus' ministry is one that challenges the economy of relationships and social conventions of his time, and ushers in a different way of being, shaped by the values of the kingdom. It is both completely new, and a return to the principles set in Exodus through manna in the desert and instructions in the law for the life of a community that would care specially for the vulnerable – the orphan, the widow, the alien and the poor.

Jesus is invited for a meal, a social occasion organised by a leader, to which those of status would have been invited. This is the background to the parables. These occasions were rife with powerplays. Who sits where, who speaks, who is nearer the host, who is invited and who is left out, all of this mattered greatly, because it was a way of reinforcing social norms and cementing one's place in society. Meanwhile, others were invisible – women, children, servants. In the Greco-Roman world, people who were poor would not have been invited to banquets; they would likely have served. Those with visible disabilities were sometimes brought in at the end for the entertainment of the guests. Here, Jesus reverses all expectations; first by arguing that meals should not be about status, power and enforcing social boundaries; second, he offers a vision of meals where the uninvited, those who usually serve, are guests reclining at the table, with as much status as the host.

It isn't a coincidence that the final parable speaks of guests who refuse to attend. It comes after Jesus told his hearers to invite 'the crippled, the lame and the blind' (v. 13). People of status would not want to attend a banquet where that was a possibility. Ironically, their refusal makes space for more of those they considered undesirable. In the end, the host commands that all should be invited. There is space in the kingdom of God for all to enter, and for all to sit together.

3 Eating with sinners

Luke 14:25—15:10

Chapter 14 focused on undermining the social rules that placed some at the top and others at the bottom, including a religious pecking order that had the obviously 'religious' at the top and sinners at the bottom.

Chapter 15 picks up the theme and explores it further, through three 'parables of the lost': the lost sheep, the lost coin and the lost son. The prompt for the stories is Jesus eating with sinners. We're still talking about meals! Jesus does not buy sinners' favour, nor does he condone their sin, and still they are drawn to him. Onlookers thought Jesus would be defiled by doing this. But Jesus turns their logic on its head. Instead of accepting their premise that uncleanness and sin are contagious, he models contagious holiness. He reverses the direction of travel: do not isolate from sinners for fear they will contaminate you; rather, spend time with them so they can grow closer to God.

Jesus goes even further: don't just associate with those who seem far from God, actively go out looking for them! He then launches into the parable of the lost sheep, drawing on rich biblical imagery of God as Israel's shepherd (Psalm 23), and of the dangers of wicked shepherds (Ezekiel 34).

Jesus surprises his hearers from the start: 'Which one of you... go after the one [sheep] that is lost'. Traditional ways of speaking do not cast blame, so Jesus would have been expected to say, 'if a sheep is lost'. Instead, he highlights the responsibility of the shepherd for the loss. His parable is, in part, about leadership. Shepherds are responsible. They must model active, compassionate care that goes the extra mile. They should always be vigilant, and if a sheep gets lost, they must do anything in their power to locate them – even though it may be dangerous for their own life. To come back to the wider setting, those who refuse to spend time with sinners, to journey with them and help them, play a part in 'losing' them.

Yet at the same time, there is irony in the parable, since the subtext, clearly, is that Jesus' detractors, who think themselves 'holy', are not immune to being lost. Therefore, when Jesus sits at table with them, he is in fact eating with sinners and reaching out to the lost.

4 The two lost sons

Luke 15:10–32

The story of the prodigal son is so well-known that it is easy to gloss over it. Yet even its title masks its richness. Set in its context of chapter 15, the story, like that of the lost sheep, is also an answer to the complaint that Jesus eats with sinners, and it pulls at the same thread: who is a sinner? Who is really lost?

Right from the start, this is a story of a father and two sons; not of one son, with a bit-part for the other. The family dynamics between all three underpin the whole story. The elder son would have been entitled to a larger portion of the estate. He would also have had more honour than his younger brother. The younger brother speaks to the father as one who wishes his father was dead, because he wants to inherit now. His words effectively break the relationship, yet the father yields, and by yielding, refuses to break the relationship from his end. At this point, a responsible older son would normally have been seen to plead with his brother, reason with him, perhaps try and mediate. But the older son is silent. He shows no emotion at the loss of his brother. The two may be lost in very different ways, but there is no doubt that *both* are lost.

The story progresses but does not quite finish. We never know whether the younger brother really changes his ways, or whether the older brother sees sense. The lost sons are both in the house of the father, but both face the choice of how to be part of the family there. They can walk out. We never know to what extent the relationships are mended. The younger son came back out of necessity. The older son fails to see what has been his all along, and his attitude shows that he does not value his father's love much more than his younger brother did at the beginning. Which son is more lost? Will they turn to the father, and realise his countercultural, overwhelming love and grace? The story does not say – and the question is left for Jesus' hearers to ponder for themselves.

5 Dishonesty, cleverness and grace

Luke 16:1–18

This parable in chapter 16 is in some ways the exact opposite of those in chapter 15. We barely know it, we rarely preach on it, we might even feel a little embarrassed by it. What does it mean? Is Jesus commending dishonesty?

We need to read this in continuity with the parable of the father and his two sons. In both there is a gracious man, who holds wealth but is generous with it, and a scoundrel who seeks to dispossess him. Both parables tell us something far more important about the master/father than about the sons/steward.

The steward is probably an estates manager of a large farm. When found to be dishonest, he offers no excuses and does no pleading – an unusual response. His silence is a tacit acceptance of guilt. The master's response is unexpected too. He dismisses the man, but does not throw him in jail or sell him into slavery to recoup his losses. He treats him both justly and generously.

The steward is concerned with getting another job ('be received in other houses'), so he reduces debt by enormous amounts (a year and a half's salary for a farm worker). The recipients do not know that he was dismissed, and must simply assume the master is being generous. The steward assumes that if he is found out, the people can claim they were not complicit, because they did not know he was fired, and ask for the reduction to be honoured, but will feel loyalty to him for helping them.

The master then is left with a choice: pursue his money and lose his reputation, or live up to the generosity that people ascribe to him. He chooses the second, but also deals with the steward. He tells the truth. The steward is exposed – so he will be watched. But he is declared 'clever', so he will likely find employment.

The steward is not praised for being dishonest. Indeed, he is called a 'child of this age' rather than a 'child of light' (v. 8). He will need the mercy of others to be helped, not his cleverness. It is the master's character that is at the centre – holding together justice and mercy in his response to both steward and community.

6 The cost of indifference

Luke 16:19–31

Chapter 16 closes with yet another parable that addresses social injustice, the power of wealth and the call for disciples to heed the teaching of the law on how to live well as communities. The message is straightforward, but small details give depth and texture to the story.

Lazarus is the only character ever named in Jesus' parables; his name means 'God is my help', which seems ironic in light of his circumstances. Yet in death, he finds comfort, and the rich man longs to become the one who is helped, but finds that he is not. When Lazarus lay at the rich man's gate, waiting for leftovers from the rich man's banquet, food was given to the dogs. Dogs were not beloved pets but symbols of wildness and uncleanness, yet they were treated better than Lazarus. Dogs lick their own wounds, and the people they love. Here they lick Lazarus' wounds, in a gesture that shows they care more about Lazarus than the rich man does.

When the scene shifts to a heavenly realm, it would be easy to think it is a simple reversal of fortunes; but the text is not so crude as to suggest that if you have a good life you go to hell, and a bad life, to heaven. Instead, the story shows that even when faced with torment and evidence of his hard-heartedness, the rich man still does not get it. He demands that Lazarus be sent to help him, when he had never helped Lazarus. He still treats Lazarus as inferior, and does not address him directly. Instead of reflecting on why he finds himself where he is, he uses being a descendant of Abraham to try and get help. His mind is totally shaped by fixed ideas of class, status and privilege. Even when confronted by Abraham, he still cannot see what the problem really is, does not apologise to Lazarus or acknowledge his own hardness of heart.

The story exemplifies how deeply wealth and status can affect our ability to see the world for what it is, and to respond in ways shaped by the gospel. Not all rich men are baddies in Jesus' parables – there are masters who become servants, others who act generously and fathers who forgive. The key with all of them is that they turn privilege into blessings for those around them.

Guidelines

One narrative strand in the gospel of Luke is the hiddenness of God and the gospel to those who are not shaped by the values of the kingdom. They look for God in the wrong places, seek to serve God in ways that bring pain to others and fail to address their own sin. Jesus' teaching on discipleship is not simply about habits of life, but shapes our ability to see where God is at work, and how to join in. How do you hone your ability to discern God? How does this happen in your church?

It is difficult to read this middle section of Luke and not notice quite how much of Jesus' teaching focuses on wealth, status and social justice. Just like the Old Testament prophets, Jesus highlights that there is no worship, no holiness, outside of an integrated life that displays the values of the kingdom, and the values of the law: both of those seek to give shape to a community where all can flourish, all can eat their fill, and where there is no hoarding at the expense of others. This isn't just a challenge for individuals, but a challenge to entire communities. How does your church or local community of faith address this communal challenge, in teaching, prayer and action?

FURTHER READING

Kenneth Bailey, *The Cross and the Prodigal* (IVP, 2005).

Kenneth Bailey, *The Good Shepherd* (SPCK, 2015).

Henri Nouwen, *The Return of the Prodigal Son* (Darton, Longman and Todd, 1994).

Keys to transformation in Titus and Philemon

George Wieland

How does the gospel affect transformation in people, households and communities? The two letters we shall read this week offer some answers.

It has been conventional in New Testament scholarship to query the authorship of the letter to Titus on the grounds that it seems to differ from the Pauline *Hauptbriefe* (Paul's 'main letters' such as Romans, 1 Corinthians and Galatians) in some items of vocabulary, theological statements and tone. It is often interpreted as a product of a later stage in the development of the church, addressing issues of church order, heretical teaching and the place of the church in society. In this scenario, writing in Paul's name claimed the apostle's authority, but the people and places mentioned merely give the impression of real correspondence and do not represent the actual situations of the letters.

This week, however, we shall attempt a reading of the letter to Titus that does take seriously its stated destination of Crete as a mission context. Against the background of the social and religious characteristics of life on Crete at the time when Paul and his colleagues were active, the apparent oddities of the letter begin to make sense. An outline emerges of creative missional engagement with Crete's distinctive culture that envisions gospel transformation within that society.

The authorship and situation of Paul's letter to Philemon, a Christian slave-owner in Asia Minor, is rarely questioned. What troubles contemporary readers is the apparent lack of moral outrage at the institution of slavery. Why would the apostle of freedom send a slave back to his master? In the mission context of the Roman world, however, this short letter appeals for a remarkable transformation of relationships that, ultimately, the social structures would be unable to contain.

Unless otherwise stated, Bible quotations are taken from the NRSV.

1 Transformative hope

Titus 1:1–4

Ancient letters were rarely private in the modern sense, even when addressed to an individual. They would have been read aloud and heard not only by the named addressee but also by their household and others. Accordingly, when a person in authority wrote to someone to whom they had delegated responsibility, it served both to instruct the recipient about their role and to authorise them in the eyes of their community to fulfil that role.

From 2 Corinthians, we see that Titus was a significant member of Paul's team, trusted to represent the apostle in challenging situations. He was a Greek and uncircumcised (Galatians 2:2–3), a living testimony to the inclusion of Gentiles among the people whom Christ has redeemed. Paul addresses him as his 'true child in the faith we share' (v. 4), suggesting that Titus had received that faith through Paul's own ministry.

There is an engaging personal story of encounter, relationship and cross-cultural partnership here, but Paul sets his story and that of Titus within an infinitely larger perspective. He sketches the outline of God's saving purpose from its beginning 'before the ages began' to its fulfilment beyond the horizon of time in the gift of 'eternal life' (v. 2). That purpose is being realised now, in this *kairos* time of opportunity, through the proclamation of God's message (v. 3) producing faith, knowledge of truth and lives that please God (v. 1).

God 'never lies' (*apseudēs*, v. 2). The conviction that God is without deceit is pervasive in Jewish and Christian faith (e.g. Psalm 89:35; Hebrews 6:18), but the term *apseudēs* is unusual, found nowhere else in the New Testament. Why here? The Cretans had a reputation in the ancient world for deception (v. 12). The term *kretizein* (to act like a Cretan) had entered the Greek language as an expression for acting craftily. But this was also a characteristic of the great god of the Cretans, Zeus, with whom they claimed a unique relationship. The problem, as Homer's *Iliad* illustrates, was that Zeus was a 'lover of lies' (*philopseudēs*) who could not be trusted to do what he promised.

Transformation requires not only dissatisfaction with the present but also a secure hope that orientates towards a different future. That is the transformative hope that the gospel offered to the people of Crete.

2 Transformative leadership

Titus 1:5–16

The gospel had reached Crete some time before Titus served there as Paul's delegate. Members of Crete's long-established Jewish community were in Jerusalem on the Day of Pentecost (Acts 2:11), and they would have returned with accounts of what they had experienced. As the faith spread around the Mediterranean world, news would have continued to reach the island through the regular sea traffic, particularly on the corn route between Egypt and Rome. We can infer that as he went around this 'island of 100 towns' (Homer), to 'every town' (*kata polin*, v. 5), Titus would have come across many groups of believers.

Titus' role, then, was not to begin mission work on Crete but to 'put in order what remained to be done' (v. 5). The urgent need was for leadership that would nurture those young churches in their life, faith and witness. A range of terms is used to describe the ministries that were to be exercised. *Presbyteroi* (elders, v. 5) were respected community leaders, valued for their understanding and wisdom, who embodied the character of the new community. An *episkopos* (bishop/overseer, v. 7) exercised supervisory responsibility. That term is paired here with *oikonomos* (household manager, v. 7), reminding us that local churches gathered in homes and functioned as extended households, requiring practical administration. There is no suggestion of a hierarchy. It is not even clear if the oversight/management role was to be a separate appointment or simply elaborates on the kind of responsibility elders had to fulfil. The concern is not to establish a particular ecclesial structure but to ensure that each of the mission churches is faithfully cared for and represented in its community.

How were such leaders to be recognised? Paul's advice is to look at their everyday lives. What qualities – or defects – of character are revealed in their home life, their relationships with others, including strangers (*philoxenos*, v. 8), their speech and behaviour? Are they respected outside the group or open to justified criticism? They should certainly have a secure grasp of the Christian message and be able to provide 'healthy teaching' (a better translation than 'trustworthy word of the teaching') and bring correction where needed (v. 9), but it was those who exemplified transformation in their own lives who would offer truly transformative leadership.

3 Transformative lifestyle

Titus 2:1–10

The typical household in the Greco-Roman world comprised the head of the household, usually (but not always) male, wife, children and slaves. How to manage such a household was a common topic of discussion, and moralists developed 'household codes' listing what was expected of each category. A number of such lists are found in the New Testament (Ephesians 5:21—6:9; Colossians 3:18—4:1; 1 Peter 2:18—3:7; and here in Titus 2:1–10). Although they have some similarities in form and content to those of the Greco-Roman writers, they all have distinctively Christian features, aligning everyday behaviour with allegiance to Christ, a fuller degree of mutuality and a concern for witness.

Among them, the instructions in the letter to Titus follow a most unusual pattern. In the standard form, obligations were set out in pairs of relationships within a household (wives-husbands, children-parents, slaves-masters). In Titus, however, behavioural instructions are given to senior men (v. 2), senior women (vv. 3–4), young women (vv. 4–5), young men (v. 6), Titus himself (vv. 7–8) and slaves (vv. 9–10). This actually corresponds to a very distinctive social structure on Crete, a throwback to the warrior culture of ancient Sparta. Travel writers commented on the coarse environment of the *andreia* (men's halls) where the men ate communally and seasoned warriors received privileged treatment. Cretan boys were separated from their families at a young age and organised into *agelai* (herds) for a programme of military-style training. They joined the men in the *andreia* where their aspirations and attitudes were shaped by the conversation and examples of the older men. For women, the tedium of a life largely restricted to within the household could be relieved by gossip and excessive drinking.

In that social environment the lifestyle instruction in the letter represents not passive conformity but radical difference. For new believers to remove themselves from the pervasive socio-economic system was not really an option. Rather, Paul asks them to learn to live differently within that structure. Older men could model a gracious, loving masculinity; women could exercise a priestly role (*hieroprepēs*, v. 3) as they taught the way of love in their households; slaves, seemingly powerless, actually had the power to give a beautiful demonstration of the teaching about a saving God (v. 10). In this way, their countercultural lifestyles would become transformative within the structures of Cretan society.

4 Transformative power

Today's section of the letter includes two highly significant – and unusual – theological statements (2:11–15; 3:4–7). The concept of epiphany, an appearing or manifestation of the divine, plays an important role. The coming of Christ into the world was an epiphany of God's grace (2:11) and love (3:4). Believers await a further epiphany of Christ in glory (2:13). In the present age, the epiphany continues in the manifestation of God's promise of life through human messengers (1:3).

A surprising feature is how the saving effect of grace is described: it is 'training us' (*paideuousa hēmas*, 2:12). Specifically, it teaches us to say no to ungodly impulses and desires and choose instead self-control, right behaviour towards others and a desire to please God, in marked contrast to the lying, brutality and self-indulgence for which Crete was notorious (1:12). On the acropolis above the town of Gortyn, Crete's Roman capital, stood a shrine to the Cretan goddess *Potnia Thērōn*, the 'mistress of beasts', revered for her ability to tame wild animals. Evidence has been found of cultic offerings on that site comprising clay figures of youths in armour. It is likely that the help of the goddess was sought as the 'herds' of boys completed their training and were transitioning to adulthood. Could she use her powers to bring them under control? Grace is presented in this context not only as God's willingness to forgive what people have done but as a power that trains and forms them for life of a wholly new quality.

In Roman times, the Egyptian goddess Isis was worshipped around the Mediterranean, including Crete. Her temple in Gortyn's public square included a baptismal pool where an annual ritual that evoked the flooding of the Nile was enacted. Initiates stood under gushing water, hoping that it would generate new life and they would emerge with a new identity as devotees of the goddess. That practice seems to be reflected in the unusual description of God's saving effected by 'the water of rebirth and renewal by the Holy Spirit [whom] he poured out on us richly through Jesus Christ our Saviour' (3:5–6). There were evidently people on Crete who longed for transformation. The message for them was that it was indeed possible through the transformative power of the Saviour God's intervention.

5 Transformative goodness

Learning in oral cultures depends on memory, aided by various devices. One such is a chiastic structure (from the Greek letter *chi* that looks like a capital X), whereby a unit is constructed in an A-B-C-B-A pattern, with a series of ideas moving towards a central point and a corresponding series flowing from it. The statement about salvation in verses 3–7 is in that form:

    A. What we were (v. 3)
      B. God's action – the appearing of God's goodness (v. 4)
        C. Key fact – God saved us (v. 5)
      B. God's action – the Spirit was poured out (vv. 5–6)
    A. What we now are (v. 7)

Extending the chiasm, the account of God's saving is bracketed by exhortations to live out that salvation by doing good (vv. 1–2, 8). Theology and practice are fully integrated.

'Doing good' is a major theme of this letter. A church leader had to be a 'lover of goodness' (1:8). People who were 'unfit for any good work' were not to be trusted as teachers, no matter what knowledge of God they claimed to have (1:16). The 'sound instruction' (2:1) spelled out what doing good would mean in practice in various life-settings (2:2–10). Older women were to 'teach what is good' (2:3) and Titus himself was to be a 'model of good works' (2:7). The purpose of Christ's self-giving was to redeem a people 'zealous for good deeds' (2:14) who were therefore to be 'ready for every good work' (3:1). Titus' teaching was to develop believers who would 'devote themselves to good works' (3:8, 14).

The Saviour God's message for the island of Crete was stunning. A trustworthy God promises eternal life; God's grace and love have appeared in space and time in the person of a Saviour, Jesus Christ, who gave himself for us; real transformation is possible by the power of the Holy Spirit. As we have seen, this message had to be formulated in such a way that it could be truly understood within the religious and cultural world of Crete. But it had to be seen as well as heard. That was the commission given to the new churches around the island. As God's saving transformation worked in them, they were to be present in every part of their society as agents of transformative goodness.

6 Transformative identity

Philemon

At first glance, this short letter contains neither theological exposition nor ecclesial advice. It is peppered with 'I' and 'you' statements, as if Paul and Philemon were standing there face to face. But others are listening in. With Paul are Timothy (v. 1), Epaphras (v. 23) who had brought the gospel to Philemon's region around Colossae (Colossians 1:7–8; 4:12–13), Mark, Aristarchus, Demas and Luke (v. 24). With Philemon are 'our sister Apphia' (Philemon's wife and/or a church leader), Archippus, active in ministry (Colossians 4:17) the members of the house church meeting in Philemon's home (v. 2), and, of course, Onesimus, the returned slave (vv. 10–12). So this letter does concern the whole church, with radical implications for its internal life and its impact on the wider community. It is also profoundly theological in the basis for its appeal.

It is commonly assumed that Onesimus had run away, having stolen to fund his escape, got into trouble and encountered Paul as a fellow-prisoner. But none of that is in the text. In the context of the current debate in the United States over reparations to descendants of slaves, that negative representation of Onesimus has been challenged. Historically, it served the interests of Christian slave-owners to make the slave the wrongdoer rather than the one wronged. What if Onesimus been sent by Philemon to assist Paul in prison, arriving not as a thief but as a trusted envoy? It can be revealing – and chastening – to ask who benefits and who suffers from any particular interpretation of the Bible.

Paul's letter is a master class in persuasion – affectionate, respectful, tactful, witty – but the foundation of his appeal is identity. Who is Paul? Prisoner, old man, father in faith, partner, but above all, brother (v. 20). Who is Philemon? Coworker, household head, church patron, but again, brother (vv. 1, 20). Who is Onesimus? Slave, child in the faith, valued helper, but most importantly, brother (v. 16). They and those listening in are being challenged to recognise each other across social and economic distinctions as siblings belonging equally within the family of God. Doubtless there would have been challenges: loss of power for some, personal and relational discomfort, resistance from a society threatened by such disruption. But the obstacles, then and now, must be overcome through leaning into the reality of that transformative identity.

Guidelines

- *Do you know your neighbourhood?* The letter to Titus demonstrates a deep knowledge of the people and places of Crete. How well do you know your neighbourhood? Take time to walk around. What – and who – do you see and hear? What do the people among whom you live put their hope in? What are their aspirations for their families and community? What kind of transformation do they long for? Pray, asking God how God's promise and gift of life could reach those places and people.

- *Do you know your church members?* What are the life situations of the people with whom you worship? What challenges do they face in living grace-taught lives in those everyday contexts? Consider how your church could resource them for that.

- *Do you know your family in Christ?* Pray that you may recognise your sisters and brothers in Christ, particularly those who are different from you culturally or socioeconomically. What will it mean to relate to them more authentically as your family members? Take the first steps.

FURTHER READING

Michael Barram, Drew G.I. Hart, Gimbiya Kettering and Michael J. Rhodes (eds), *Reparations and the Theological Disciplines: Prophetic voices for remembrance, reckoning, and repair* (Lexington, 2023). See chapters on Philemon by Angela N. Parker and Michael J. Gorman.

George M. Wieland, 'Roman Crete and the Letter to Titus,' *New Testament Studies* 55 (2009), pp. 338–54.

David C. Wright, *Integration: A conversation between theological education and the letters to Timothy and Titus* (Langham Global Library, 2022).

Joshua: possessing the promise

Leoné Martin

The book of Joshua charts the emergence of Israel as a nation. Joshua is chosen to lead a new generation out of the wilderness into the land that Yahweh had promised but that the previous generation had failed to possess. Joshua is called to complete the mission his predecessor Moses was unable to finish because of a moment of disobedience (Deuteronomy 3:23–28). Through successes and failures in battles, Yahweh teaches Israel what it will take to possess his promises.

It can be challenging to reconcile the God who commands and sanctions violence in the Old Testament and the God who suffers violence himself to save us in the New Testament. It's therefore important to acknowledge that while the book of Joshua deals with Israel's conquest of the promised land and the deposing of other nations, it is not a blueprint or licence for conquest or colonialism. As Amy Orr-Ewing states, 'The coming of Christ and the beginning of the New Testament institute a new era in a biblical understanding of battle' (Orr-Ewing, 2020). In this new era, the battle is not for physical territory, and geographical borders do not define the promised land. Jesus made it clear that his kingdom is not of this world (John 18:36).

Nevertheless, Joshua is a challenging read for many. The violence it records can be unsettling, but as a significant period in the history of Israel and a crucial episode in salvation history, it is vital that we accept the invitation to wrestle with the questions it raises and the truths it reveals. After wrestling, we will not have all the answers, but hopefully, we will have a deeper revelation of who God is and who we are called to be as his people.

Unless otherwise stated, Bible quotations are taken from the NRSV.

1 Be strong and courageous

Joshua 1

The encouragement to 'be strong and courageous' is given four times within Joshua 1. In three instances, it is spoken by Yahweh to Joshua (vv. 6, 7, 9), and the fourth time, it is spoken by the people to him (v. 18). Humanly speaking, Joshua had much to fear. Yahweh called him to lead the nation in a liminal period, emerging out of the wilderness and into the promised land. The land was not abandoned but occupied by fierce foes whose presence had intimidated a previous generation into rebelling against God's command to possess the land. The nation had just finished mourning the death of its founding leader, Moses, and was entering a new chapter in its history and formation. Joshua was now called to occupy Moses' leadership position, continuing the mission in a new phase.

The task was undoubtedly daunting for Joshua, yet Yahweh had promised to give the nation this land as their inheritance. While Yahweh was sovereignly at work, bringing to pass the promises made to the patriarchs, he chose to work through human agents responsible for responding to his commands. In this instance, Joshua was his chosen instrument. God declares, 'For you shall lead this people to possess the land that I swore to their ancestors to give them' (v. 6).

However, the successful possession of the promised land was conditional; obedience to Yahweh would be the pathway to the promise (v. 8). This generation was called to break the cycle of disobedience, correcting the mistakes made by the previous generation who got stuck wandering in the wilderness for 40 years because of their fear. Thus, internalising the instructions of Yahweh so that they could be faithfully followed was a vital component of the nation's prosperity (v. 8). Their obedience would secure their success and serve as a witness and reminder for the generations to come.

Yahweh not only reassured Joshua with the promise of success and prosperity but also with his presence. Joshua needn't fear because 'the Lord your God is with you wherever you go' (v. 9). Yahweh would be with Joshua like he was with Moses. Human leadership responsibility may have transitioned, but Yahweh was still overseeing the unfolding mission.

2 An unlikely heroine

Joshua sends two spies on a similar reconnaissance mission as the one he had been sent on years earlier. While this time the mission has a positive outcome, this is not because of the spies' personal success or competency but because of the intervention of an unlikely heroine. Verse 2 reveals that these spies spend the night in the house of a prostitute called Rahab. It is unknown why they chose to lodge in this woman's home or whether they were there for unsavoury reasons, but it seems a strange and inappropriate place for servants of Yahweh to find themselves while on a mission to carry out his commands.

As soon as they enter the land, their identities and movements are detected. Their mission is communicated to the highest authority in the land, the king of Jericho, who immediately sends word to Rahab to give the men up. Then the story takes an unexpected twist; rather than giving the spies up, Rahab conspires to conceal the spies and betray her country. Her actions amount to treason. She knows these men are part of a nation that plans to destroy her own. So why would she ally herself with them?

Some may take the cynical view that this is a sinful woman who merely looks out for her own interests. However, as she negotiates the salvation of herself and her family, interesting insights are revealed about her view of Israel's God. She says, 'The Lord your God is indeed God in heaven above and on earth below' (v. 11). This woman with a questionable occupation acknowledges Yahweh as the one true God and aligns herself with his purposes by offering aid to his people. The text has an uncomfortable tension, as Rahab must lie and betray her nation to save the spies. Interestingly, Rahab is not criticised for lying. As this account is recalled by New Testament writers, her actions are commended as an act of faith (Hebrews 11:31; James 2:25). Through Rahab's shrewd advice and action, the spies escape capture and are bolstered by reports that the inhabitants of Jericho's 'hearts melted' because of them. Yahweh's use of an unlikely ally rescued what began as a failed mission.

3 Crossing over

Joshua 3

Finally, the day to exit the wilderness and enter the promised land had arrived. Joshua functioned not only as Israel's military leader but also as their spiritual leader. Part of Joshua's spiritual function was to act as a prophetic voice to the nation, relaying Yahweh's instructions. Obedience to the instructions Yahweh gave through Joshua would make the difference between success and failure, life and death. The people were told to follow the ark carried by the Levitical priest so that they would be able to navigate this unfamiliar territory, and they were also warned to keep their distance. The final leg of their journey into the promised land was dangerous; not only did the overflowing banks of the Jordan present danger, but the presence of Yahweh in the camp also posed a threat if not handled correctly. For Israel, Yahweh's presence among them in the form of the ark of the covenant was both essential and dangerous.

Yahweh promised to perform a miracle before them that day. In the same way that a water miracle led them into the wilderness when the nation crossed the Red Sea on dry land, now a water miracle would take them out of the wilderness as they crossed the Jordan on dry land. This miraculous event would serve three primary purposes. It would establish Joshua as a competent leader in the eyes of the people (v. 7); it would prove that Yahweh was the living God, and it would act as a guarantee of Yahweh giving them victory over their enemies in the promised land (v. 10).

The crossing of the Jordan on dry land was not a private miracle. It took place in the sight of the nation of Israel and of the surrounding peoples. Verse 16 tells us that the waters 'stood still, rising up in a single heap far off at Adam', beside the city of Zarethan. Supposedly, the people dwelling in these places would have witnessed this strange phenomenon if not the actual crossing of the nation of Israel. The time of crossing is also significant. Verse 15 indicates this was the harvest time when the Jordan overflowed its banks. There could be no doubt that the parting of the waters was an act of Yahweh. Through obedience to and faith in Yahweh's words, the entire nation successfully crossed the Jordan on dry ground and entered the next phase of its development as a nation.

4 Remember

Joshua 4

The crossing of the Jordan was such an important milestone in the nation's history that Yahweh commanded Joshua to set up a memorial that would be a lasting reminder of his faithfulness to Israel. Sizable stones were to be claimed from the midst of the Jordan, carried by twelve representatives from each of Israel's tribes and set up on the border of the promised land. This memorial would act as a conversation starter for future generations. When inquiries were made about the significance of the stones, future generations could be educated on the faithfulness of Yahweh in allowing the nation to cross the Jordan on dry land. The vital task of developing a national memory of Yahweh's power and faithfulness is reinforced by the repetition of, 'When your children ask…' (vv. 6, 21).

Verse 9 indicates that Joshua also set up a second memorial amid the Jordan, covered by the flow of its waters once Israel crossed over. The function of this monument appears to be less emphasised in the text. Nevertheless, it acted as a marker of where the priest stood, carrying the presence of Yahweh as the nation passed by.

Verses 12–13 act as a stark reminder of the task that lies ahead of the nation as they make their miraculous and triumphant entry to the promised land. Around 40,000 warriors go ahead of the people. Though it was Yahweh giving them the land, they would have to engage in battle to possess it. However, the memorial stones would act as a reminder not only for future generations but also for the present generation that Yahweh keeps his promises.

Verse 19 highlights that Israel crossed over on the 'tenth day of the first month'. This timing is significant as it marks the date of the Passover, Yahweh's final plague that compelled Pharaoh to let the nation go, liberating them from 430 years of enslavement. Linking the memorial stones with the institution of the memorial of Passover reinforces the important role that remembering will play in the nation's prosperity. Notably, the scope of the sign was not limited to Israel but was so that 'all the peoples of the earth may know that the hand of the Lord is mighty' (v. 24).

5 The first victory: the fall of Jericho

Joshua 6

The first battle Israel engages in when the people enter the promised land is against the fortified city of Jericho. The inhabitants are shut up inside, presumably afraid and sheltering behind the walls for protection. However, the walls are no match for the power of Yahweh. After following Yahweh's unconventional battle strategy, of circling the wall once for six days and seven times on the seventh day while seven priests blew trumpets, the wall supernaturally fell. Israel rushed in and secured their first battle victory in the promised land.

The description of the entire city being devoted to destruction – with no living person or animal left alive other than Rahab and her family – is troubling. It can be challenging for contemporary readers to comprehend why Yahweh would sanction, command and facilitate acts of violence on this scale. While this violence is difficult to reconcile, it is important to note two things. First, Yahweh called Israel to be a nation that modelled life under his rule and reign. Second, there was fluidity between those devoted to destruction and those Yahweh chose. Joshua's warning to Israel in verse 18 makes clear that by disobeying Yahweh's instructions concerning the devoted things, Israel herself could become 'an object for destruction'.

The salvation of Rahab and her family further indicates that the lines between those devoted to destruction and those classified as Yahweh's people were not fixed. The inhabitants of Jericho would have received the same information as Rahab about Yahweh's dealings with Israel and the wonders he had performed. However, it appears that this did not result in the same revelation. While Rahab acknowledges Yahweh and aligns herself with his plans in faith, the other inhabitants of Jericho rely on the walls for protection. As a result, miraculously, though Rahab's home is in the wall that falls, she and her family are rescued and brought to safety while the city perishes.

Israel's first victory in the promised land was won not by military prowess or sophistication but by careful obedience to Yahweh's commands. While Joshua might be the human commander-in-chief, it is Yahweh's battle-plan that he is following. Jericho was to be a positive case study for how to win future victories as they conquered Canaan. Through these battles, Yahweh was not only giving them the land but, more importantly, teaching them how to live as his people within it.

6 One man's sin, communal consequences

Israel's victory over their enemies is short-lived; after the resounding success of Jericho, they are hit by the bruising defeat at Ai. Previous success made the Israelites overconfident in their abilities, leading them to rely on human intelligence-gathering rather than depending on the divine insight and assistance that secured their last victory. They fail to consult Yahweh before engaging Ai in battle, sending fewer fighters, who end up running away, with 36 being killed.

Joshua is devastated by the defeat and lies in mourning before Yahweh with the elders. Yahweh rouses Joshua from his lament with a sharp rebuke and reveals that the nation has sinned by taking things devoted to destruction, something that could have been revealed had Joshua consulted Yahweh before going into battle.

Though one man had sinned, guilt is attributed to the entire nation. Due to this guilt, they cannot succeed in battle. Western sensibilities may bristle at the idea that a whole community suffers the consequences of one man's disobedience. However, this idea is not so foreign or unthinkable in cultures that are more communal than individualistic. It is understood that the actions of one can both positively and adversely affect the lives of the whole.

The judgement pronounced on Achan that results in his whole household being burnt along with all his worldly possessions highlights the gravity of violating the covenant Yahweh had established with Israel. Achan's choice made Israel vulnerable; they had become 'a thing devoted for destruction'; they could no longer win against their enemies; and Yahweh would no longer be with them. The only way to regain Yahweh's presence and protection was to destroy the devoted things in their midst (v. 12).

This episode in Israel's history would act as a cautionary tale (22:20). Achan hoped he could hide his sin and get away with it, but Israel was shown that what could be hidden from each other couldn't be concealed from Yahweh. Though Yahweh chose them, their unique relationship came with weighty responsibilities and their rebellion against him would make them no better than other nations. They could not rely on national identity, past success or military numbers; only their faithful obedience to Yahweh would guarantee possession of the promised land and their prosperity within it.

Guidelines

Faith is an undercurrent in the book of Joshua. Only by faith in Yahweh and his ability to fulfil his promises will Israel be able to possess the land fully. While Yahweh has chosen Israel as his means of blessing the nations, even in this formative stage in their development as a nation, it is faith that distinguishes those who are part of his chosen people as opposed to those who are devoted to destruction (*cherem*). Through faith in Yahweh, Rahab, a prostitute and Gentile, escaped destruction, gaining salvation for herself and her family. It is by a lack of faith in Yahweh and rebellion against him that Achan became *cherem*, leading to destruction for him and his family. This thread of faith points towards the ultimate fulfilment of salvation through faith in the person of Jesus Christ. Jesus said, 'If you love me, you will keep my commandments' (John 14:15). True love for and faith in God inspires faithful obedience to his commands, and obedience is the pathway to all he has promised.

- How might Yahweh's encouragement to be 'strong and courageous' to Joshua encourage us in our participation in his mission?

- How do these early chapters of Joshua shape your understanding of faith and what it looks like to be faithful to God?

- What might we learn about the consequences of disobeying God's instructions and its impact on the success of our participation in God's mission?

- How does the idea that Yahweh's presence was both essential and dangerous to Israel shape your understanding of God? How might this shape our appreciation of God's indwelling of believers through the Holy Spirit?

- How do you feel about the violence contained in the book of Joshua? What questions does it raise for you?

See the further reading list on page 49, which includes resources that delve deeper into ways to understand the violence in the Old Testament, including the book of Joshua.

1 Conquest

Joshua 11

Chapters 10 and 11 of Joshua can be seen as some of the most unsettling passages of scripture as they record violence commanded by Yahweh that can be hard to reconcile from our contemporary perspective. However, as the fulfilment of frequently restated promises not only to Moses and the nation of Israel but also to the patriarchs stretching back to Abraham (Genesis 15:16), they form an essential aspect of salvation history.

Verses 16–23 summarise Israel's battle victories against both the southern and northern kings. Although the records of these battles detail what appears to be a rapid conquest, verse 18 makes it clear that Israel was engaged in a sustained military campaign over an extended period. The statement, 'So Joshua took all that land', at the start of verse 16 may give the impression that Israel's work was done, but as David Firth observes: 'There is a great deal of difference between taking the land and occupying it' (Firth, 2021). Though the land now had rest from war (v. 23), Israel would still need to do the hard work of allotting the inheritance and establishing themselves as a nation.

The link between victory and obedience is a repeated theme throughout the book of Joshua. Joshua destroyed these nations, and won these victories in response to the command that Yahweh had given Moses and that Moses had passed on to him. Though Joshua and Israel may have been the means of victory, success came ultimately from Yahweh. It was Yahweh who hardened the hearts of their enemies so that they did not seek peace but initiated warfare against Israel. Thus, when Israel engaged in battle with the armies of the northern kingdoms, it was in defence. The language of 'harden[ing] their hearts' is reminiscent of the hardening of Pharaoh's heart when he resisted Yahweh's command to let his people go from captivity in Egypt. Rather than Yahweh being the cause of their rebellion, it is better understood as him giving them over to their wicked inclinations.

In verses 21–22, the triumph over the Anakim is specifically singled out. The imposing size of these people caused the previous generation to shrink back in fear of entering the promised land, but now this generation had conquered them, just as Yahweh had promised.

2 A work in progress

Joshua 13:1–7

As Joshua grew older, the nature of his involvement in Yahweh's mission would have to change, and so would how Israel was led. Joshua had to prepare the nation for when he would no longer be with them. We see a shift from centralised leadership focused on national figures like Moses and Joshua to the tribes empowered to possess the land allocated to them. Yahweh raises the issue of Joshua's age and reminds him of the land still to be possessed and the task of allocation outstanding. There is no indication that advanced age is a disqualification for leadership. Moses led Israel until his death at 120 years old. However, as Joshua approached the later years of his life, it was vital that he refocused his priorities and finished his part of Yahweh's mission of giving the promised land to Israel. Allocating the land before all the region's inhabitants were driven out was an act of faith. Joshua and Israel would need to trust that Yahweh would continue to fulfil the promises made to them. Again, the emphasis is placed on the action of Yahweh; it is Yahweh who would drive these nations out of the land (v. 6).

Firth again notes the distinction between taking the land and occupying the land (Firth, 2021). There were instances where the land would need to be retaken, and it would be each tribe's responsibility to drive out the inhabitants of the land allocated to them. For example, in verse 4, land belonging to Aphek is listed as land still to be possessed, but in Joshua 12:18, the king of Aphek is listed as one of the kings defeated by Joshua and the Israelites. Possessing the land fully would take time, commitment and continued obedience. In Exodus 23:30, Yahweh warned Israel that their enemies would be driven out 'little by little… until you [they] have increased and possess the land'. While Israel achieved many battle victories, the allotment of territory did not mark the end of their fighting. Although the land enjoyed a period of rest from war (11:23), each tribe would need to fight again with Yahweh's help to occupy the land given to them fully (see chapter 12).

3 Wholehearted

Having distinguished himself, along with Joshua, as one of only two spies to give a positive report after their spying out the promised land 45 years previously, Caleb stands out once more as an example of faithfulness and obedience. As soon as he realised the time had come to divide the land, he seized the opportunity to possess the territory promised to him. Caleb demonstrated an understanding of the balance between human responsibility and divine enablement. Although Yahweh gave him the city, he must act in faith to possess it.

The hill country promised to Caleb was an extremely challenging territory to take. It was a fortified city where the Anakites lived. Verse 15 draws attention to the fact that this city used to be called Kiriath-arba (city of the four), named after Arba, 'the greatest man among the Anakim' – highlighting the danger and difficulty involved in capturing this location. These men of giant proportions were the same people who inspired fear in the Israelites and caused ten of the twelve spies to rebel, giving an unfavourable report.

Yet Caleb did not allow the difficulty of possessing the land to deter him. As difficult as the task of driving out giants from a fortified mountainous region may have seemed, he knew it was possible with Yahweh. Avoiding or neglecting to completely drive out the inhabitants may have seemed easier in the short term. However, this would have devastating consequences in the long term if Israel succumbed to idol worship.

Chapters 14—19 detail the allocation of the land among the tribes of Israel. Several times, it mentions the failure of certain tribes to completely drive out the land's inhabitants (15:63; 16:10, 17:12–13). Caleb's obedience and attitude to the promises of Yahweh serve not only as a contrasting example to those who rebelled against the will of Yahweh but also those who only partially fulfilled his commands. The word translated as 'wholeheartedly' in the NRSV is mentioned three times in verses 6–15 and means 'to the full'. Caleb left nothing undone of what Yahweh commanded; he followed the instructions to the full. Caleb's complete obedience, faith and determination were rewarded, as 15:14 records that Caleb drove out the descendants of Anak.

7–13 October   45

4 Altar of witness

Joshua 22:10-34

When Joshua dismissed the eastern tribes, their actions before crossing over the Jordan to their inheritance put the nation of Israel on the brink of civil war. The Reubenites, Gadites and half-tribe of Manasseh build an imposing altar and word about this travels, sparking outrage among the other ten tribes. They immediately conclude that the eastern tribes have rebelled against Yahweh and must be destroyed. Mercifully, they follow the guidelines set out by Moses for when the apostasy of a town or region is suspected and send a delegation to investigate the matter (Deuteronomy 13:14).

The approach taken by this delegation in confronting the eastern tribes is certainly not a template for conflict resolution. Rather than seeking to understand their reasons for erecting the structure, they lead with a barrage of accusations based on their assumptions about why the altar was built. They conclude that the eastern tribes have forsaken Yahweh either by turning to serve other gods or by offering sacrifices in an unauthorised location, violating the law (Deuteronomy 12:13-14).

While their approach was questionable, their motivation was sound. They understood that although separated from the eastern tribes geographically, they were one nation united under a covenant with Yahweh. Thus, rebellion by the eastern tribes would bring judgement and devastating consequences for the whole nation. They cite two examples from Israel's history when the many suffered for the transgressions of the few. One was the plague that broke out at Peor due to Israel's engagement in sexual immorality and idol worship, resulting in the loss of 24,000 lives (Numbers 25:1-9). The other was the more recent example of Achan and the ensuing defeat at Ai.

The eastern tribes' response swiftly defuses this fraught encounter. They assure the delegation that the replica altar was not fashioned for idol worship or unauthorised sacrifices but is a reminder that though the tribes are geographically divided by the Jordan, they are united in worship to Yahweh. Anxiety that future generations would be excluded from participation in worship and thus turn their backs on Yahweh was their motivation for this symbolic structure of witness. The initial reaction to the altar of witness and the exclusionary language of referring to the ten tribes as the 'whole congregation' in verse 16 is indicative that their anxieties were not entirely without foundation.

5 Passing on the mission

As Joshua approaches the end of his life, Israel approaches another period of transition and change as a nation. Just as Moses had shared parting words with the nation, passing on leadership responsibility to Joshua, it comes time for Joshua to do the same. This time, rather than passing on leadership to a national figurehead who would act as both military and spiritual leader, Joshua passes on leadership responsibility to tribal representatives (elders, heads, judges and officers). Although verse 2 states Joshua 'summoned all Israel', the leaders are specifically highlighted.

While Joshua has successfully led the taking and allotment of the promised land, it is clear that the mission of fully possessing and settling in the land still needs to be completed. A remnant of the previous peoples remains (vv. 7, 12). This reality indicates that devoting these nations to destruction did not necessarily mean the death of every inhabitant but could suggest dismantling their national identity, establishing in its place a nation within this region under the rule and reign of Yahweh. However, this would depend on the people of Yahweh maintaining their distinctiveness and not succumbing to the temptation of assimilating the evil practices of the previous nations.

In his farewell speech, Joshua implores the nation to 'hold fast' to Yahweh (v. 8). The Hebrew word *dabaq* can also be translated as 'cling'. The same word is used in verse 12 but is rendered as 'join' in the NRSV to warn Israel not to cling or cleave to the remnant of the nations that remain among them through intermarriage. The implication is clear: if Israel clings and stays close to Yahweh, they will continue to possess and prosper in the land; conversely, if they cling to the survivors of the enemy nations, worshipping their gods and imitating their practices, then they will lose their identity, becoming like them and forfeiting their inheritance. As Joshua passes on the mission at the end of his life, he reminds the nation that their distinctiveness and success are predicated on their faithful obedience to Yahweh. Just as Yahweh has been faithful in bringing about the blessings of obedience, he will be equally as faithful in bringing about the curses of rebellion (v. 16).

6 Who will you serve?

Before his death, Joshua gathers all of Israel at Shechem, where he renews the covenant. Shechem is significant, as it is where Abraham (then Abram) built an altar to Yahweh when he first arrived in Canaan (Genesis 12:6–7). Yahweh had been faithful in bringing to pass all the promises he made to Abraham and the other patriarchs. In the first 13 verses, Yahweh speaks through Joshua to recount their history and his faithfulness from Terah (Abraham's father), who served other gods, to the conquest of the promised land. The point is that Yahweh himself has given them the land as he promised long ago. Now that they are living in the land that was promised, they have a choice to make. Will they faithfully serve Yahweh, who has chosen them, delivered them out of slavery and given them the land they have not laboured to develop, or will they serve the gods of their ancestors, Egypt and other local deities?

The threads of faith and obedience woven throughout the book of Joshua culminate in Joshua's declaration, 'As for me and my household, we will serve the Lord' (v. 15). Having started as Moses' assistant, by the end of the book Joshua is granted the same illustrious title as Moses: 'the servant of Yahweh' (v. 29). He has proved his faithfulness and he calls the nation to do the same. The people respond with the correct answer; they pledge allegiance to Yahweh, but this response does not satisfy Joshua. He disputes their ability to serve Yahweh, highlighting his attributes of being holy, jealous and just. The crux seems to be that while they profess allegiance to Yahweh, in practice, some still worship other deities. Twice Joshua implores the nation to 'put away' other gods, indicating an issue with idolatry (vv. 14, 23). Joshua emphasises that this is a dangerous and destructive path. Yahweh will not share the loyalty and affection of his people.

As the nation affirms their commitment to serve Yahweh, Joshua calls them as witnesses against themselves. He also sets up a stone as a witness and reminder of their commitment. Verse 31 indicates that they lived up to this commitment while the elders who had been eyewitnesses to what Yahweh had done lived, but as the book of Judges shows, this commitment was not maintained by subsequent generations.

Guidelines

Joshua led a new generation of Israel to succeed where the previous generation had failed. They crossed over from the wilderness into the promised land, took possession of the land, allotted each tribe their inheritance and began to settle within it. What previous generations had longed to see and hoped for from afar, they experienced. However, possessing the promise was not once-and-for-all-time; possession had to be maintained. In the same way, obedience was the pathway to the promise; obedience and loyalty to Yahweh would be the means of holding on to it. The survivors of previous nations would test Israel's loyalty to Yahweh. Would they maintain their distinctiveness by remaining faithful to Yahweh, or would they succumb to the temptation of idolatry?

While we may not be tempted to worship physical idols, anything that replaces devotion to God is an idol. Money, power, popularity and sex are common contemporary 'gods' that tempt us to worship and devote ourselves to them. Jesus warned, 'If any wish to come after me, let them deny themselves and take up their cross and follow me' (Matthew 16:24). Although we are now under the new covenant of grace, we are still confronted with the question, 'Who will you serve?' While we celebrate Jesus as our Saviour, will we demonstrate our love and loyalty by obeying him as Lord? In Matthew 6:24, Jesus reminds us that we can't serve two masters; we must choose.

- What does idolatry look like in our contemporary society?

- How can the church maintain its distinctiveness amid the temptations to worship the 'gods' of the prevailing culture?

- What might Caleb's example of wholeheartedness look like in today's church?

FURTHER READING

Tony Evans, *The Tony Evans Bible Commentary: Advancing God's kingdom agenda* (Broadman & Holman Publishers, 2019).

David Firth, *The Message of Joshua* (IVP, 2021).

Amy Orr-Ewing, *Why Trust the Bible?* (IVP, 2020).

Helen Paynter, *God of Violence Yesterday, God of Love Today?* (BRF, 2019).

Hugh R. Page Jr., *The Africana Bible: Reading Israel's scriptures from Africa and the African diaspora* (Fortress Press, 2010).

Psalms Book V (Psalms 107—150): the king's people in a changed world

Bill Goodman

In our journey through the Psalms, we have encountered King David and his experience of God's covenant commitment (Books I and II); then destruction and disillusionment in Israel and Judah during the time of David's successors (Book III). This led on, through the trauma of exile in Babylon, to a renewed focus on Yhwh as the true king of David's lands and people (Book IV). Israel's story is woven into the shape of the Psalter.

Now the story continues. With some of the exiles restored to their homeland, they consider a changed and changing world. With their monarchy no longer permitted, they remain a vassal state, subservient to the Persians. Their rebuilt temple in Jerusalem lacks the grandeur of its predecessor and daily life is still full of struggles. How can they cope with these disappointments and their sense of being oppressed, still feeling partly 'in exile'? What does it mean to preserve their identity as a people in such circumstances? Book V highlights these questions. It gives glimpses of a rationale for existence and a renewed sense of national identity, focused on Yhwh as their true king, rather than David's line or any of the empires around them.

Book V contains different voices. Within it we notice some obvious collections, such as those titled 'Song of Ascents' (120—134) and two groups introduced by the call to praise, 'Halleluia' (111—118; 146—150). Meanwhile David, who largely disappeared in Books III and IV, re-emerges in two groups entitled 'David's' (108—110; 138—145). At the heart of the book stands a massive celebration of Yhwh's instruction (119). We need to consider how all this fits together and what kind of hope for the future it offers – to its original hearers and also to us in our day, in our own changed and changing world.

Unless otherwise stated, Bible quotations are taken from the NRSV.

1 Celebrating the experience of ḥesed

Psalm 107

Book V of the Psalms begins with reminders of how Book IV ended. Psalm 107 shares the same opening words as Psalm 106, along with other phrases such as 'wonderful works' and 'rebels'. Above all, the word ḥesed (Yhwh's faithful, covenant love) is again emphasised, appearing at the start and end of Psalm 107 and in each of the four refrains – this psalm could be seen as a sermon on the nature of that ḥesed (which will appear again in 108:4; 109:21, 26 and other psalms that follow).

Book IV closed with a plea for God to gather his people from among the nations (106:47). Book V begins with clear echoes of those words, indicating that the plea has been answered (vv. 1–3). This psalm celebrates and gives thanks for that saving, restoring work of God, depicting it for us in four brief examples.

These four scenarios include vivid details, which could evoke the experience of release from exile in Babylon (or before that, the exodus from Egypt). In spite of people's waywardness, God's grace has continued and still continues in their present situation. So let them remember and rejoice in what Yhwh has done and testify to Yhwh's acts of commitment.

The imagery in these four case studies also turns them into open paradigms, which echo other experiences of trauma down the centuries, including our own today. Many can relate to feeling lost in a parched desert, imprisoned in oppressive darkness, cut down through your own foolishness or about to drown in a storm-tossed sea. Any who do are invited to join in the pattern of response repeated throughout: to acknowledge their distress, cry out to Yhwh, experience God's saving action – and then give thanks for it. Yet that prayer does not need to be made in an organised worship setting: it can be prayed at sea or in the desert, from a sickbed or a prison.

This great song of celebration ends with a steer towards wisdom – a theme which will recur as Book V unfolds. Here is teaching through testimony. God's people need to attend to testimony and learn wisdom, as they press on into their new future.

2 Malediction

Benediction means speaking good of people or to people, such as a prayer of blessing at the end of a worship service. In this psalm we find the opposite – malediction, proclaiming the bad, uttering a curse or an imprecation.

In Psalm 109 we hear shockingly negative words spoken about others. There is provocation – the psalmist is responding to verbal attack. The move from 'they' to 'him' (vv. 1–5 compared with vv. 6–19) may indicate that this section of the psalm is quoting what the enemies say against the psalmist, rather than vice versa. But even if so, the verses that follow (vv. 20, 29) show the psalmist taking up these words of his accusers and asking God to bring these same curses on them. We find this kind of prayer in a few other psalms (e.g. 58:6–9; 69:22–23; and most notoriously, the end of Psalm 137).

Psalms such as these remind us that injustice happens – and it provokes anger. If suppressed, that anger can breed apathy, self-blame or indifference to what is wrong. The challenge is how to handle such anger. Are we invited to share in the sufferer's hatred, or simply in their pain? Perhaps in some traumatic situations, genuine forgiveness and resolution can only come after a genuine articulation of outrage – or even hatred?

The psalmist's words are directed to God, not at the offender. As we saw in Psalm 94, anger is expressed forcefully – in prayer – and then entrusted and submitted to God. God is not asked to empower the speaker to attack their enemies; indeed, these are not the words of a powerful figure leading a vigilante group, but of one who senses their own powerlessness. Here is prayer, hope, yearning; but action is left to God. This violent-sounding prayer proves in fact to be an act of non-violence: a prayer that protests against violence, not one that approves of violence.

Along with expressions of outrage and hatred, the word ḥesed, which we noticed repeatedly in Psalm 107, recurs again (vv. 12, 16, 21, 26). This emphasis on Yhwh's faithful, committed love remains clear, even amid the anguish and anger. Psalm 109 does not end with hatred of enemies but with a renewed focus on Yhwh and an expression of trust that God will act justly.

3 The mysterious priest-king

Psalm 110

'An oracle of Yhwh': these striking opening words (here translated 'the Lord says'), found only here in the Psalms, are very common at the end of pronouncements in the Old Testament's prophetic books. Does this indicate that Psalm 110 should be interpreted as prophetic? Numerous interpreters down the years have understood it that way.

This divine oracle presents a mysterious 'lord', first as a royal figure (vv. 1–3), then also as a priest (vv. 4–7). These roles come together in a priest 'after the order of Melchizedek' – a mysterious figure whom we meet briefly in Genesis 14:17–24, who has authority to bless even someone as distinguished as Abram. Melchizedek somehow carried authority in both the political and religious spheres, founded on his righteous character – the name means 'King of righteousness'. Divine authority and power are given to this 'lord', says our psalm, enabling him to defeat all his enemies (vv. 1–2, 5–6).

Yet ancient Israel wisely avoided putting too much power into one pair of hands; combining the roles of priest and king in one person was not permitted. So who is this priest-king 'lord' in Psalm 110? Could it be King David? This psalm, along with the two that precede it, is entitled 'David's'. It might have been written originally for the coronation of David or one of his successors. Placing it here in Book V, where the return from exile is in view, is suggestive: Israel under Persian rule is no longer permitted to have a king – yet the presence of this coronation psalm challenges that fact, indicating that God's promises to David and his successors are not simply forgotten.

Yet none of those Davidic kings in Jerusalem were also priests – still less ones as powerful and awesome as depicted here. From the earliest times, Christians have seen this psalm as prophetic, pointing to Jesus Christ ('great David's greater Son', as one of our hymns puts it). The New Testament quotes this psalm ten times. Jesus uses it to challenge his critics to acknowledge his authority (Matthew 22:41–46). Hebrews 7 expounds at length how Jesus is the fulfilment of Psalm 110's priestly Melchizedek figure. Later commentators follow suit: Calvin declares that Psalm 110 is 'a very clear prediction of the divinity, priesthood, victories and triumph of the Messiah', while Luther's commentary on this one psalm runs to 123 pages!

4 The wise acts of God – and the wise human response

Psalms 111—112

Halleluia, the call to praise Yhwh, features as the opening headline throughout this group (Psalms 111—118). Traditionally known as the 'Egyptian Hallel', these psalms are used in the Passover festival, as Jewish people remember and celebrate Yhwh saving them from slavery in ancient Egypt.

Psalms 111 and 112 mirror each other like non-identical twins, with much shared vocabulary. They form a pair of very compact alphabetic acrostics (each line beginning with a successive letter of the Hebrew alphabet). This form may have been used to aid memorisation and/or perhaps to express the presence of order and completeness, an A–Z of wisdom.

In Psalm 111, Yhwh's splendour and holiness, faithful actions and covenant commitment (111:5, 9) are all acknowledged and praised. How does that divine character and wisdom then impact the world? Psalm 112 answers this question, underlining that human wisdom begins with awe and reverence for God (111:10; 112:1). It shows us a proper response to all that God has done, in language that reminds us of Psalm 1. The righteous one who behaves wisely is *ashrē*, meaning 'content' or 'fortunate' (the opening phrase of both Psalms 1 and 112) and delights in Yhwh's teaching (112:1; compare 1:2); while the wicked are doomed to perish (the final word in Psalms 1 and 112).

One significant aspect of this wise and righteous living is the right use of wealth in commitment to those who are poor, particularly by those who are significantly better off (112:3, 5, 9); sharing resources with those who lack them is evidence of one's attachment to Yhwh.

The words 'grace' and 'mercy' are paired in 111:4 – declaring what God is like; they are repeated in 112:4 – showing what a wise and righteous human being is like. This pair of words is used in the great self-declaration of Yhwh's character in Exodus 34:6–7 (a passage which reverberates throughout the Old Testament, as we noted when reading Psalm 103). It is through the lives of Yhwh's faithful ones that divine compassion and grace shine out into the world. The godly person of Psalm 112 draws on their understanding of the God of Psalm 111, in order to express God's character through right living and truthfulness in daily life.

5 Celebrating God's salvation

Some of the psalms have an intensely personal feel, with a single, consistent voice speaking throughout. Psalm 118 is different: multiple voices seem to speak at different times, with some repeating and others responding to each other. Even the individual voice which we do hear in the middle section might be speaking on behalf of the whole community. In addition, we glimpse ceremonial actions involving the opening of gates and processions to the altar. It has the feel of a lively liturgy used in corporate worship at a festival.

Psalm 118 rounds off this 'Egyptian Hallel' group (111—118), traditionally used, as we noted earlier, in celebrations of the Passover festival. That Passover connection is seen in phrases in Psalm 118 suggesting the exodus story of the Jews escaping from slavery in Egypt (particularly Exodus 15). Yet that imagery could also suggest a more recent victory in battle – or the end of exile in Babylon and return to the promised land, which was sometimes depicted as a new exodus.

One intriguing image in this psalm is the spurned stone (vv. 22), which a group of builders initially rejected as unsuitable (perhaps due to its size or shape) – but later realised was just what was needed, as a foundation joining two walls together or perhaps at the top of an arch. The psalm declares that this is what happened to Israel (or a particular leader of Israel): spurned and dismissed contemptuously by the nations, yet eventually finding a more exalted position than anyone could have imagined.

Yet these words may feel familiar. Like Psalm 110, this psalm is much quoted in the New Testament, whose writers found new significance in its verses, which helped them make sense of what God was doing in their day. The image of the rejected stone which becomes the cornerstone is used repeatedly about the rejection, death and resurrection of Jesus (Mark 12:10; Acts 4:11; Ephesians 2:20–21). In addition, all four gospel writers link Psalm 118 with Jesus' triumphal entry into Jerusalem, where the crowds shout the words *Hosa-nah*, meaning 'save us, we implore you' and 'blessed is the one who comes in the name of the Lord' (vv. 25–26; see Matthew 21:9; Mark 11:9–10; Luke 19:38; John 12:13). Our lectionaries offer Psalm 118 for Palm Sunday and Easter Day.

6 The way of Yhwh's teaching: an A–Z

Psalm 119:1–8, 81–88, 169–176

In Psalms 111 and 112 we encountered very concise alphabetic acrostics. Now we discover the most expansive acrostic of all, with the first eight verses each beginning with the opening letter of the Hebrew alphabet, the next eight verses with the second letter and so on. Here is the ultimate A–Z of what it means to delight in Yhwh's *torah*/instruction (v. 1). Almost every line refers to Yhwh's teaching, word, commands, judgements, etc. Frequent mention of a 'way' or 'path' underlines that this is the celebration of an ongoing spiritual journey, centred on divine instruction and on the God who has given it.

What kind of psalm is this? The inventive poet offers praise, testimony, protest, confession, plea – all kinds of prayer, moving between them apparently at random – but all as part of the focus on God's teaching. This *torah* is not a burden, but a delight (vv. 14–16). The speaker commits to understanding and walking in Yhwh's way; yet also senses a great need of divine help in order to do so (vv. 33–36).

Links with the Wisdom tradition, which we noticed in Psalms 1, 19 and 111—112, are evident in this psalm also. The opening words strongly echo the beginning of Psalm 1; but the godly individual of that psalm now becomes a godly community (vv. 1–3). Yet a very personal sense of relationship with Yhwh also pervades this whole psalm: worshippers come as individuals as well as in a corporate body.

We find no mention here of temple, priesthood or sacrifice. Perhaps this reflects a time during or soon after the exile, when there was no Jerusalem temple and study of God's *torah* became a crucial way for the devout to preserve their worship and identity.

The speaker is thrilled by Yhwh's teaching (vv. 97–104). But not everyone is equally enthused: some resist it, scorning and attacking those who seek to walk in it. This prompts a sense of sadness and anger; of feeling secure in God, yet also vulnerable – to internal weakness, which leads to straying from the truth, and to external attack from others (vv. 84–86). Repeatedly the speaker pleads for God to give 'life' (for example, vv. 25, 40, 154, 156, 159, 175). Having begun with assurance and delight, this psalm closes with lament and perhaps a sense of uncertainty – a tension that is not resolved (v. 176).

Guidelines

Did one of these psalms particularly catch your attention? If so, explore the reasons why. Is there something about it which stands out for you?

In Psalm 107 we see people calling to God in times of desperation: recognising their need, crying out for help, experiencing God's rescue and giving thanks. How do the four scenarios depicted in this psalm resonate with your experience and that of the church down the years? Perhaps things you have heard and experienced can prompt you to rejoice in God's continuing commitment to the church, in spite of its many weaknesses and failings.

For those of us who are not suffering abuse and persecution, the words of Psalm 109 might feel embarrassing or deeply disturbing. For those elsewhere who are suffering such traumas, they might feel like a lifeline, perhaps also a pathway to genuine hope for the future. Who can you think of and pray for who might find this psalm meaningful at the moment?

We've noticed how much Psalms 110 and 118 feature in the New Testament. How much do the Psalms feature in the worship and preaching in your church(es)?

In Psalms 111 and 112, we noticed the importance of knowing God's character and then expressing it in our daily lives. Can you find a verse or phrase in each of these psalms which particularly resonates with you and your ministry at the moment?

One of the likely aims of acrostics is to help worshippers memorise the words. In the coming week, why not try memorising a short verse from each day's psalm? You can then feast on that verse at different moments in the day, perhaps even murmuring it to yourself, as the psalmists encourage us to do, day and night (1:2)!

In Psalm 118 we heard various voices speaking out in corporate worship. Are you able to hear different voices contributing in your church's worship? Are any voices missing or underrepresented?

Psalm 119 expresses delight in God's teaching. Is there a Bible verse or passage that has delighted or excited you recently? Can you find an opportunity to share that verse and your experience of it with others?

1 On the way up

Psalms 120—124

In Jewish tradition, Psalms 111—118 are traditionally used as part of the spring celebration of Passover, while Psalm 119 is used at celebrations of Pentecost. Now we find another group of psalms (120—134), used during the autumn feast of Tabernacles (or Booths, Sukkot), a festival focused on Israel's journey through the wilderness after the exodus from Egypt. The various liturgical elements, professions of faith and benedictions in this group make them particularly suitable for a festival celebration.

Each of these 15 psalms is headed 'A Song of Ascents', probably suggesting pilgrims going up to Jerusalem (see 122:4; compare 24:3); the city's name is mentioned in a number of them, as is Mount Zion, the site of the temple. Or if translated 'A Song of the Steps', these headings might evoke worshippers inside that temple complex, climbing a particular series of steps as part of drawing near to God (compare Ezekiel 40:6).

There seems to be a flow in their order. In Psalm 120, Jerusalem is not mentioned, with the distressed speaker depicting life far from home among hostile people. Then in Psalm 121 we find ourselves on a journey, looking (perhaps anxiously) at the hills, where bandits may lurk, ready to rob unwary pilgrims; yet perhaps also looking ahead towards Mount Zion, the destination and reminder of Yhwh's presence and help. With Psalm 122, we arrive at an idealised Jerusalem (or else anticipate arriving) and admire the great city, praying earnestly for its peace and prosperity. The next action after arrival is to look to God and seek God's help: life is still full of threats and challenges (Psalms 123—124).

We don't know when each of these short psalms was written. But gathering them and ordering them in this part of Book V links them to the return from exile. Those Jews who returned from Babylon faced many problems, including local opposition and ridicule, as the books of Ezra and Nehemiah testify. Their small community in Jerusalem remained at the mercy of stronger political powers, not least their Persian overlords. Little wonder that they sensed so strongly a need for Yhwh to be their guard (a word found six times in Psalm 121). Yet they continue to trust and declare that Yhwh is their helper and on their side (121:1–2; 124:1, 6–8).

2 The hope of David

Psalm 132

The Songs of Ascents are all brief and thus easy to memorise – apart from this one. Its greater length makes it stand out, as does its content and position. It continues the focus we have noticed on worship at Mount Zion, the location of the temple in Jerusalem. But now we face up to an issue which those returning from exile had to make sense of: the absence of a Davidic king on the throne in that city of David.

Set between two psalms headed 'David's', Psalm 132 talks directly about David, mentioning him four times. It revisits the memory of his project to locate the Ark, the symbol of Yhwh's presence, in Jerusalem (1 Chronicles 13—16). It reaffirms the importance of Zion as Yhwh's chosen dwelling and resting place, as Yhwh has declared and promised (vv. 5, 8, 13–14).

The need for continued obedience is highlighted, hinting at the reason why Yhwh brought about the end of the royal line (vv. 11–12). Yet the psalm closes with hope for renewal of God's grace and of human response in worship (vv. 15–16) – leading to hope that a powerful new Davidic king would somehow emerge (vv. 17–18). Does the psalmist speak on behalf of those who are expecting a literal fulfilment of this hope, which will end Persian imperial rule? If so, they did not see that expectation fulfilled. Christians see this hope finally fulfilled in the coming of Jesus, the royal 'Son of David' (Matthew 21:4–9).

Hopes and expectations may well have varied among the post-exilic community. But this psalm continues to declare that there is one true king in Zion – Yhwh. The new temple may have been built with Persian resources and blessing; but Zion remains the place for the worship of Yhwh, who is still the 'mighty one' of his chosen people (vv. 2, 5, 8). Yhwh's greatness can never be contained in one small place; yet that divine presence residing in Zion, even in the lesser temple rebuilt after the exile, is a sign and an assurance to the faithful in Jerusalem. This ultimate king is the one who directs the affairs of earthly kings, makes reliable promises, raises up kings and puts down their enemies. Subversive ideas? Certainly food for thought for the Jews of Jerusalem – and even for their Persian rulers.

3 Knowing and known; assurance and anger

Psalm 139

How can such a sublime poem suddenly twist into such a disturbing ending? Wonder, assurance and security that arise from relationship with God suddenly dissolve into a violent outburst of anger against enemies, almost as shocking as the closing verses of Psalm 137. We may feel conflicted by the contrast, wanting to ignore that final disturbing section (as churches often do, omitting those final verses in their recommended lectionary readings).

A key word, found seven times in this psalm, is 'know'. Not the head knowledge of 'knowing about', but rather the language of relationship: the relational dance of 'I' and 'you' language is abundant throughout. In the first section (vv. 1–6), the speaker – an individual or a voice representing Israel – finds identity in that relationship with God; delights in the assurance of being intimately known by God in every action and feeling, desire and motive – and accepted. Realising this feels miraculous, incredible.

But does God's all-seeing eye and all-following presence feel truly reassuring? It could feel oppressive, prompting an urge to run away and hide in some remote place; the ambiguity in the second section (vv. 7–12) suggests mixed feelings, perhaps sometimes a dread of God's attentive presence and scrutiny. Yet trying to hide proves futile; so openness and honesty are the only realistic option.

Moving on to the third section (vv. 13–18), assurance returns, with a sense that, from the very beginning of the speaker's life, God's touch has been gentle and creative: like a potter, steadily and firmly moulding the clay into a pleasing and useful pot, or like a weaver, carefully and skilfully guiding the threads, creating a garment of strength and richness.

The change in tone from verse 19 onwards is sudden and bewildering. Passion for God boils over in a volcanic outburst against those who are violent, malicious opponents of Yhwh; hatred is expressed repeatedly. Realising that Yhwh already knows all prompts this level of honesty: what would be the point in trying to hide these feelings? Yet this outburst leads on to an awareness that questions self: might this passion for truth and justice be twisted by anxiety or self-pity, tainted by self-deception and a vindictive streak? The closing verses voice this possibility, as they echo the opening ones: God who has searched and known the speaker in the past is invited to search and examine the thoughts of the heart afresh (vv. 23–24).

4 The king acclaims the King

Psalm 145

The Psalter's final group of psalms titled 'David's' ends with this poem, uniquely called 'David's praise'. Praise to Yhwh is one of its major features, emphasised in the opening and closing verses. St Augustine opens his 'Confessions' with a quotation from verse 3, declaring that human beings cannot experience contentment apart from praising God, 'because you made us for yourself and our hearts find no peace until they rest in you'.

Much of the psalm celebrates the wonder of God's actions. In the first part (vv. 1–13), the focus is on Yhwh's mighty and awe-inspiring deeds of power, experienced by all creatures. In the second part (vv. 14–21), this awesome and glorious cosmic ruler becomes closer at hand, supporting those who stumble, upholding and feeding them, listening, saving and being close to those who love and cry out to God. God's greatness and God's goodness interweave throughout; that greatness expresses itself in acts of goodness.

Yhwh's goodness and greatness is highlighted in phrases that echo repeatedly throughout the Old Testament, not least in the psalms. They are first heard in Yhwh's self-revelation to Moses (Exodus 34:6–7: see Psalms 25:6–7; 86:15; 103:8; 111:4 – and now here, v. 8). God's nature and character abounds in grace and compassion, long-tempered patience and faithful commitment.

This is the last of the Psalter's alphabetic acrostics, a structure which emphasises completeness and comprehensiveness. It might have been placed here as the Psalter's last word, before the final group of praise psalms (146—150) was later added. Another of its striking features is the constant repetition of the word 'all', which is found 17 times. Yhwh is always good and to be praised at all times. God's commitment is to all of creation – not only to all humans, who are cared for and invited to respond, but also to 'all that he has made… all your works… all flesh' (vv. 9, 10, 21).

In this, the last of 'David's' psalms, there is no focus on David or his successors as king. Instead, this David repeatedly highlights God's kingship and royal rule (vv. 1, 5, 11–13). This theme features most strongly in the psalm's central verses: Yhwh's sovereignty is central, both structurally and theologically. For Jews still under Persian rule in their promised land, this might feel poignant, yet also reassuring. Human rulers and power structures may come and go, but God's rule endures and outlasts them all.

5 A better vision for leaders

Psalm 146

As if in response to the previous psalm's last verse, Psalm 146 launches the Psalter's closing 'Hallel' group. Each of these final five psalms begins and ends with *Halleluia*, which means 'all of you, praise Yhwh'. The book's title in Jewish tradition (*Tehillim*, 'praises') is underlined in this climactic surge of praise. There are also links in these psalms to the way the Psalter began, as phrases from Psalms 1—2 recur in this grand finale.

After beginning by exhorting and committing self to praise, the speaker suddenly warns against putting faith in 'princes/nobles' (vv. 3–4). There is a suggestive vagueness in this critique of human power: it might make us think of King David or one of his successors, or the Jewish elite or their Persian overlords in the time after the exile (compare 118:8–9; 144:7–8; 147:10). The exaltation of human kings found in some of the earlier psalms (e.g. Psalms 2, 21, 45, 72) has disappeared; instead, we are reminded that even the most powerful and influential are limited in their power, fallible and mortal, just like the rest of us.

Instead, help and hope are to be found in someone else (v. 5). Notice how many times the name of Yhwh is repeated in the verses that follow – Yhwh is the one to turn to, for Yhwh is the one who acts; Yhwh is the creator of heaven and earth, the sea and all the creatures in them (a theme that will continue in the psalms that follow this one). Yhwh is also powerfully active in the present. God's way of using power is to strengthen those who lack power; these verses remind us of Yhwh's longstanding commitment to the most vulnerable, summarised as 'the sojourner, the widow and the fatherless' (v. 9; compare Exodus 22:20–22; Deuteronomy 24:19–22).

Here is a vision of a society where truth is treasured and justice enacted for those who have been denied it; where food is available for those who most need it, where the most vulnerable are supported, empowered, liberated, where goodness is valued and corruption firmly resisted (vv. 6–9; compare 144:12–15). This is God's vision for flourishing – which God's people need to embrace and live out. Food for thought for us, just as for those living in Judea after the exile when some were choosing to exploit the vulnerable (see Nehemiah 5).

6 Finale

We entered the psalter through a gateway or overture (Psalms 1—2), which introduced the importance of receiving Yhwh's teaching and submitting to Yhwh's rule. Now, in this finale (Psalms 149—150), we hear again a call to respond to that divine rule and divine teaching.

Psalm 149 echoes Psalm 2, warning that rebellious nations and kings who refuse to submit to Yhwh will be called to account and face divine justice. But the task of implementing God's reign on earth, assigned in Psalm 2 to the Davidic king, is now transferred to the whole people of God (the 'saints/faithful', mentioned three times, 149:1, 5, 9). They are addressed in royal terms as those who are adorned (or crowned) in 149:4. Refuge and strength are found in Yhwh, not in a Davidic king or any other unreliable earthly kings (compare 2:12; see also 146:3–4). The opening call to 'sing a new song' to Israel's king (149:1–2) reminds us of Psalms 96—98, where the kingship of Yhwh was proclaimed and celebrated so powerfully.

The familiar terms of a psalm of praise are suddenly displaced by vivid and disconcerting imagery of swords and vengeance (149:6–9). Are God's people called to violent conquest? Hardly an option for those living under Persian rule, who were not permitted to have any kind of army. Those addressed here are the weak and powerless (149:4).

Throughout this psalm we find the kind of parallelism in which the second line of each verse builds on and develops the idea in the first line. So the two-edged swords in the second line of verse 6 must be linked with the praises mentioned in the previous line. Declaring God's praises is the way God's people triumph. We hear echoes of Moses and Miriam leading a celebration of victory over their enemies – victory won by Yhwh, acclaimed there for the first time as Israel's king (Exodus 15:7, 11, 18).

The final word is simply a stirring call to praise (a word found 13 times in Psalm 150). This is the calling not only of humans but of all creatures in the heavens and the earth (150:1, 6; compare 148:4, 7). Tambourines, dancing and singing again remind us of Israel's beginnings (Exodus 15:20). The right response to all that Yhwh has done is joyful self-abandonment, expressed together in a crescendo of praise.

Guidelines

- Does a sense of being pilgrims today shape your own spiritual life and that of your church? Look for ways in which these psalms can help.

- Pray for those who come to mind in positions of leadership, in the church and in wider society. Pray for yourself in your own leadership and the ways you use power, perhaps at work, in church or at home.

- Sometimes, rather than preaching on a psalm, it can be refreshing and helpful to pray through it, as a kind of meditative sermon. Psalm 139 works well this way, with the first section read aloud (vv. 1–6), followed by meditation/reflection on those verses, and so on.

- The Lord's Prayer echoes many themes in Psalm 145. Try praying both together and notice the connections. Could this be one of the prayers that inspired Jesus when he composed his prayer for his followers?

- How does God actually do what's described in Psalm 146:7–9? Do we just sit back and watch or wait for it to happen? Often God chooses to act through human beings; we become part of the answer to our own prayers. This captivating vision has an edge: it demands action from us!

- Who can help refresh the sung worship in your church, particularly with songs derived from the psalms?

- Spend some time simply acknowledging and celebrating God's goodness.

FURTHER READING

William H. Bellinger Jr., *Psalms as a Grammar for Faith* (Baylor University Press, 2019).

Walter Brueggemann, *Praying the Psalms: Engaging Scripture and the Life of the Spirit* (2nd edition: Paternoster, 2008) – and Brueggemann's other works.

Nancy de Claisseé-Walford, Rolf A Jacobson & Beth LaNeel Tanner, *The Book of Psalms* (Eerdmans, 2014)

Jerome Creach, *Discovering the Psalms* (SPCK, 2020).

John Goldingay, *Psalms* (3 volumes: Baker Academic, 2005–08).

Paula Gooder, *Journalling the Psalms: A guide for reflection and prayer* (Hodder & Stoughton, 2022)

Anneke Kaai, *The Psalms: An artist's impression* (Piquant, 1999).

Esther

Helen Paynter

> 'For if you keep silent at this time, relief and deliverance will rise for the Jews from another place, but you and your father's family will perish. Who knows? Perhaps you have come to royal dignity for just such a time as this.'
>
> ESTHER 4:14

These words to Esther from her cousin are probably the best-known verses of the book of Esther. In this rousing summons, he calls the young Jewish queen to undertake an act of great courage: to put herself in danger in order to attempt to save her entire people. And Esther does. She fasts and prays, then enters the presence of the king of Persia to beg for clemency for his Jewish subjects.

The story of Esther is sometimes romanticised, represented as a 'beauty pageant' which the 'lucky' young girl 'won'. As we will see, it is no such thing. Parts of Esther's story, along with the machinations and subsequent downfall of the wicked Haman, are well-known (you can read it in chapters 4—7). Less familiar, perhaps, are the stories which begin and end the book: stories of power, of abuse, of terror. This is the lens through which I would invite you to read the book with me this week.

Throughout, I would invite you each to make connections from the ancient world to the contemporary one – because tyrants are not just those at the top of a particular form of political system. Some can be found at the head of a democratically elected government. Others are in the workplace – or in the family.

Be warned. This will not be comfortable reading. The world was a wicked place in Esther's day. The world is still a wicked place. We still need courage to stand against tyrants.

Unless otherwise stated, Bible quotations are taken from the NRSV.

1 Power and appearances

Esther 1:1–18

Tyrannical control is often maintained through its representation. We see this in at least three ways in these verses.

First, note the description of the interior decor of Ahasuerus' court: the gold and silver, marble, mother of pearl, fine linen and purple cloth. Imagine being an ambassador to that court – or a slave within it. His dominance is encoded in architecture and art. This is the aesthetic of power.

Aesthetics of power take many forms in our contemporary world. Sometimes they use great monumental buildings, statues, military parades and lavish displays of wealth. Sometimes power is displayed through the furniture layout of an office, in executive parking spaces or in the use of titles and name plates on doors. Not everyone who has these things is a tyrant, but such power displays are beloved by tyrants at every level. They are all designed to say, 'I am more powerful than you,' to intimidate and even to strike fear.

But then we read of Ahasuerus' free banquet, the lavish food and drink that is provided at the king's expense. How generous, how munificent!

So secondly, we see that tyrannical power commonly presents a face of benevolence. Tyrants tell their subjects that they love them. They pretend to be generous, kind, long-suffering and magnanimous. But tyrants take by the bucketful and give back in thimbles. The gift of a tyrant always comes with strings attached. It strengthens ties of loyalty; it establishes a debt. It is never given for the benefit of the other, but to shore up power. It is not generosity, but manipulation.

Third, note the fragility of the king and his courtiers in response to Vashti's small act of rebellion. How little it takes to bruise their egos! 'Fragility' is a term that has been used in recent years to refer to someone who easily flips into a defensive posture, who sees the smallest of issues as an insult to their pride, as a slight or as a challenge. It may have racial or – as here – gendered connotations. For the king and his officials, honour is a zero-sum game. In these economics, one can only gain status if someone else loses it. Anyone else's growth is therefore a threat.

The tyrant's control is maintained through the assertion of power, the lie of benevolence and the zero-sum maintenance of status.

2 Power to coerce

Esther 1:10–16; 2:1–4

Buoyed up by days of drinking, the king orders Vashti to appear at his banquet. Not because this will please her, but because it will please *him*. Not in order to bless her, but in order to bolster his own status. 'Look at my beautiful queen. Look what I possess.' This is another example of the aesthetic of power, this time displayed by coercion over a human body.

Reading on into the next chapter, Esther and dozens of other young women become the subject of that same urge. By the king's order, beautiful virgins are to be sought and brought to the palace. Their opinion is of no interest to him.

Tyrants today often seek power over the bodies of others, whether this is exercised through political or more direct means – including conscription to fight and die, deprivation of food or shelter, forced abortion and sterilisation, enslavement and coercive or rapacious sexual activity. The women's experience in this story bears many points of similarity with the pornography industry, which largely consists of trafficked women displayed for the purpose of the male gaze. They are bodies that are acted on by others. The story also has parallels with the prostitution industry, where women are trafficked and manipulated to pleasure some men and enrich others; bodies at the disposal of tyrants.

The men who do the king's bidding also deserve some scrutiny: Memucan who speaks against Vashti (1:16) and Hegai who oversees the treatment of the trafficked women (2:3). Both these men were eunuchs: castrated in childhood to remove their capacity to be any sort of threat to the king. Themselves subjects of royal coercion and control, now they are part of that same coercive system. This is another ruse of tyrants – to make others complicit in the abusive networks they have created.

Observing this phenomenon in the Nazi concentration camps led the Jewish scholar Primo Levi to coin the term 'The Grey Zone'. The expression refers to the morally ambiguous situation where the binary distinction between victim and perpetrator breaks down. One of the powers that tyrants have is to coerce others into moral compromise. We might draw another parallel with the manipulation of young people to act as drug traffickers, or the forced conscription of youngsters into rebel paramilitary groups.

Coercion over bodies and souls is part of the tyrant's playbook now, as then.

3 Legitimisation of power

Esther 1:19–22; 3:8–15

Those of us who have had the privilege of living in democracies all our lives can be tempted to complacency about the rule of law. We tend to assume that the law operates to keep us safe, that it is broadly good and that acts of evil will stand in opposition to law. Those who have not lived in such systems all their lives will know better. Systems of abusive power are often encoded in law rather than operating in breach of it.

Law should be a good thing, and it can be a good thing. Righteous laws contribute to the common good. We should lend our support to the making of righteous laws and behave towards them with obedience (compare Romans 13:1–7).

But law, like so many other tools, can be used for good or for ill. We should not assume that it is always benign. And here, in the court of Ahasuerus, we see the far-from-benign law of the tyrant.

Tyrants love to wrap themselves in a cloak of legitimacy. They love to find ways to legitimise the control they exercise. Political tyrants will frequently do this by the enactment of laws – laws that enshrine their own agendas.

Other tyrants will use other means. Grievous inequality can become encoded into the very structures of our societies or organisations – we call this structural violence. Even scripture can be used to lend legitimacy to a tyrant's regime. For example, the Bible has been used to support racism, xenophobia and domestic abuse. Tyrants like nothing better than to pull the strings of law, of culture, of scripture itself, in order to legitimise their actions; to say in effect, 'Move along! Nothing to see here.'

4 Power and gender

When she was a young woman, probably in her early to mid-teens, Esther experienced 'the knock on the door'. The king's soldiers came to her house – that was never good news. They eyed her up. They made her stand before them, and turned her around. They checked her for physical blemishes. They evaluated her sexual maturity.

Then they took her away. They removed her from her home, from her guardian, from her possessions, from all that was familiar and secure. And they brought her into a gilded cage. We can imagine her standing in a hall with all the other young women who had been similarly selected and brought to the palace. We imagine them having their clothes taken away – their last vestige of home stripped from them – and being given new clothes that marked them out as belonging to the king. We can perhaps imagine their bewilderment, their terror, their disorientation.

We imagine them being told the rules of the place, the confines of where they may and may not go. We imagine every bodily function being overseen by the eunuchs who were put in charge of them. We imagine the hands that were laid upon them to bathe and pluck and scrub and pumice and massage and perfume and apply cosmetics. We imagine them waiting for the rape that will surely come.

And then, one night, it is Esther's turn, and she is taken from a place that has now become familiar, along a corridor, across the courtyard and into the bedroom of the king, where she waits in fear to discover his will. And her entire body is available for his pleasure.

In contemporary terms, Esther was sex-trafficked. A conservative estimate suggests that this is the daily reality for 35 million people alive in the world today. Around 20% of them are children. The industry has an estimated market value of $99 billion per annum (see **bedbible.com/ research-sex-trafficking-statistics**).

Not every victim of sex trafficking is female, and not every perpetrator is male. Every instance is a personal tragedy and a grievous sin. Not everyone survives the experience and comes out stronger, as Esther does, in God's miraculous purposes.

5 The silence of God

You may have heard it said that God is not named in the book of Esther. The absence of God's explicit activity in this book invites us to ponder our own world and its systems and structures of power. We often do not see God visibly intervening. The eye of faith may trust that God is working, but sometimes he seems slow to act and many prayers appear to be left unanswered.

Did Esther also wonder where God had gone? His people have been defeated in battle and deported far from home. They are dislocated from their homes, living at the mercy of a capricious tyrant. Where is God? Why has he not thundered in to save his people? As the story leads towards Esther's moment of courageous choice, how does she discern the voice of God?

One part of the answer is that she hears God through Mordecai. But this is not straightforward. Esther is surrounded by voices – mostly, or perhaps even exclusively, male voices – all telling her what to do. The eunuchs in charge of the royal harem tell her what to wear, what to eat, how to behave. At the top is the king himself, whose words, once sealed in law, become irreversible.

Esther didn't have a Bible to study. It's likely that it is around this time that much of the Old Testament is being written down and compiled, but she wouldn't have had access to written texts. What Esther would have had access to are the stories of God's work in history. The words that one day would become scripture would have been told to her from her cradle. Mordecai would have trained Esther from childhood to know and speak of the Lord and the love and obedience that was due to him (Deuteronomy 6:4–7).

So Esther knew something of the character of God – that he is a saving God, that he is a redeeming God, that he is a God who made a covenant with his people and a God who is faithful to his promises. And she has the reasoning capacity which God has given her, which we see her applying to the problem.

When Mordecai asks her to approach the king, her immediate response is that it is impossible, because she will certainly die. So what makes her change her mind? I think, in part, it's because she does the maths. She risks her one life in order to attempt to save thousands of lives.

And a risk it is. For, despite the sentiments of many fridge magnets, there are very few promises of God which offer certainty *in this life*.

But Esther's knowledge of the character of God tells her that there is a fate worse than death. This is the fate of being complicit in great evil. And so, she summons her courage and declares, 'If I perish, I perish' (v. 16).

6 When power is ours

Esther 8:3–17; 9:5–10, 16

We have sped through the central portion of the story. Esther's great roll of the dice has been successful. The wicked Haman is hanged. But through this sudden and unexpected reversal of fortunes, God's people have become so powerful that those who are outside this community feel the need to pretend they are in it (8:17).

If God's people ever gain access to power, this should be *good news* for those around. But time and again in history, this is not what happens. Here, the ascendency of Mordecai and Esther spells doom for tens of thousands of their fellow citizens. This highlights for us the temptations of power; the dangers of being too close to government.

When state and church become too close, their very different priorities become intertwined, resulting in serious and harmful temptations. For the state, the temptation is to seek to co-opt the church's authority for its own agenda, for its own political purposes. The church's temptation is to permit this co-option, sweetened by the inducements of privileged status, relative protection or finance. This is a Faustian bargain. History has taught us that it is terrifying what a national church can close its eyes to if it is bribed sufficiently with power and status. It is also a fundamental misunderstanding of the way that God operates in the world. He invites his people to walk a better way (1 Corinthians 1:27–31).

The church of God on earth is a transnational, ecumenical and multiracial body. Our king is above all other rules. Our loyalty to God and our allegiance to one another trump all the idolatrous claims of the state. We have no business privileging one group over another. And the coercive instruments of the state are not permissible tools for us in advancing the kingdom of God.

In this regard, Esther and Mordecai serve as negative examples to us in the end of the book. They began well, but they end badly. In defiance of the empire, they have adopted its own tools and so have become everything that they have set themselves against. They would have done better to stay in chapter 4, willing to live or die in the pursuit of justice, rather than end up in chapter 9, presiding over the death of thousands.

Guidelines

Esther's tyrant says something like this:

> Come to me, all you who are weary and heavy-burdened, and I will take advantage of you. I will lay the yoke of my will upon you, and you will be manipulated by me; for I am single-minded in my ambition; your body will be used, and your soul will be crushed. My yoke is harsh, and my burden is intolerable.

But we know the one who owns the everlasting kingdom, and to whom all honour and worship is due. His yoke is easy and his burden is light (Matthew 11:28–30):

> Come to me, all you who are weary and are carrying heavy burdens, and I will give you rest. Take my yoke upon you, and learn from me, for I am gentle and humble in heart, and you will find rest for your souls. For my yoke is easy, and my burden is light.

At the name of Jesus, all – tyrants included – will bow the knee (Philippians 2:10).

FURTHER READING

David G. Firth, *The Message of Esther* (IVP, 2022).

Kathryn Kinmond and Lisa Oakley, *Breaking the Silence on Spiritual Abuse* (Palgrave Macmillan UK, 2013).

Scot McKnight and Laura Barringer, *A Church Called Tov: Forming a goodness culture that resists abuses of power and promotes healing* (Tyndale House Publishers, Inc., 2020).

Helen Paynter, *The Bible Doesn't Tell Me So: Why you don't have to submit to domestic abuse and coercive control* (BRF, 2020).

The politics of Jesus

Max Kramer

John Howard Yoder's book, *The Politics of Jesus*, published in 1972, awakened increased academic interest in the political implications of Jesus' life and teachings. This has been accompanied by an increased emphasis on political matters in preaching, the public pronouncements of church leaders and within the sphere of Christian activism.

This short set of reflections does not seek to summarise this large area of thinking. Instead, drawing on the gospels, it invites us to consider how we think politically as individuals who seek to live the Christian life, and to consider how as Christians we might go about the business of formulating our own political views.

The complexities of this challenge can be seen in one of the texts we often think of as the most explicitly political: the Magnificat. This song of joy is sung by Mary to her cousin Elizabeth as a response to her pregnancy with Jesus, and includes the words:

> [The Lord] has shown strength with his arm; he has scattered the proud in the imagination of their hearts. He has brought down the powerful from their thrones and lifted up the lowly; he has filled the hungry with good things and sent the rich away empty.
>
> LUKE 1:51–53

To us, these look like political statements: revolution, new regimes, relief for the poor, punishment. Yet, while political language is used, Mary does not present her song as a social manifesto. This is not necessarily something she says *should* happen. Rather, Mary proclaims that this is something that has in some sense *already happened* in salvation history and in the incarnation of Christ (the verbs are past tense), despite the fact that looking around her she would have seen a hungry people continuing under Roman rule. Exploring texts which show Jesus coming face to face with political power in teaching and experience will help us to understand better the significance of this apparent contradiction.

Unless otherwise stated, Bible quotations are taken from the NRSV.

1 Jesus the king

Matthew 2:1–18

As any clever Sunday school student can tell you, the famous carol 'We three kings' gets it completely wrong. The Bible never says there were three of them, and they almost certainly weren't kings. Nevertheless, recognising the true identity of the Magi should not lead us to ignore the importance of kingship in the opening of Matthew's gospel.

We can see this in the first verses. Herod (often referred to elsewhere by his name alone) is twice called 'King Herod', and the Magi describe Jesus not as 'Messiah' but as 'the king of the Jews'. It is hard to imagine that Herod could hear that title applied to someone else as anything other than a threat, as this title was his own, granted to him by the Roman Senate.

For Matthew's readers, however, this shared claim to a title invites us to compare and contrast the two kings that the story presents. This comparison has two dimensions, both of which are held together in one word: Matthew's assertion that Jesus was the one born (*techtheis*) king of the Jews (v. 2).

On one level, the statement that Jesus was *born* king emphasises the greater legitimacy of his rule. Unlike Herod, whose Idumean ancestry made him questionably Jewish to his contemporaries, the prophecies of the Messiah's birth, when taken together with his birthplace and his genealogy in Matthew 1, vindicate Jesus' claim to be the true king, the royal descendent of David.

Yet, the word 'born' also speaks of the difference in the nature of the kingship of the two characters. Unlike the domineering King Herod, who can summon a massacre on a whim, the newborn King Jesus is completely vulnerable, not only to the violence of Herod but also to that of Rome. This is emphasised by the many allusions to the passion that permeate this text: the title king of the Jews (used on the cross), the gathering of religious leaders as a prelude to violent acts, perhaps even the gift of myrrh.

The story of the two kings, therefore, is not the story of one powerful king or regime being replaced by another (slightly better) one, but rather the radical replacement of one kind of kingship with another – a form of kingship which is vindicated not by impressive achievements or the effective wielding of power, but by apparent failure and suffering.

2 Jesus the political teacher

Luke 20:20–40

'Is it lawful for us to pay tribute to Caesar or not?' The spies' question to Jesus is exactly the kind of political question we often hope the Bible might answer for us. Should we do X or should we do Y? Surely Jesus should give us a straight answer?

Yet, while Jesus' response does incidentally allow for payment of the tax, his refusal to engage straightforwardly with the questioners reveals that he has a larger and more important point to make. Jesus' answer not only escapes the questioners' attempted political trap, but also serves as a reprimand to their insincere approach.

As Nolland points out, Jesus' insistence that the questioner produces his own coin reveals for all to see that the questioner is happy enough to make use of the currency (for all its supposedly problematic image of Caesar) when it arrives as income. The religious scruples only arise when it comes to paying it out as expenditure. As Nolland puts it, Jesus exposes the 'convenient alignment of piety and self-interest' (p. 961) often inherent within us when we seek a religious answer to a political question.

This emphasis on insincerity is reinforced when we read this parable in its original context with the following question about resurrection. The Sadducees have no interest whatsoever in having their question answered honestly. Their only purpose in posing it is to seek to expose belief in the resurrection as ridiculous. Again, Jesus' answer emphasises the narrowness and poverty of imagination inherent in those who seek to boil down hope in the life to come to a series of practicalities.

This reading of these parables presents a challenge to us. When we seek to read Jesus simplistically as a political teacher, in this reading we hear him asking us, 'How sincere is your approach?' Do we really wish to hear his wisdom on our perplexities, or have we already made up our mind and are just seeking legitimation, or a religious rationale, for our own self-interested convictions, cherished prejudices or self-righteous ideals?

3 Jesus the potential political leader

If the question about tax tells us something about the complexities of Jesus as a political teacher, the entry to Jerusalem addresses those associated with Jesus as a political leader.

Evans notes no fewer than twelve triumphal entries into Jerusalem of which Jesus' contemporaries might have been aware (pp. 357–58). The similarities between these scenes and Jesus' entry to Jerusalem perhaps encouraged the crowd to see this new hero as a potential political saviour. Yet, Matthew's manipulation of Zechariah's prophecy reveals to the attentive reader that the view of the Jerusalem crowd is not one we should share.

After quoting the opening of Zechariah 9:9 ('See, your king comes to you'), Matthew omits the words 'triumphant and victorious is he', thus deliberately emphasising the only adjective that he leaves in: 'humble'.

Initially, 'humble' (*praus*, also 'gentle/mild') may not seem a very accurate description of the one who goes on to turn over the tables in the temple. Yet, perhaps the humility here is that Jesus does not simply replace one defeated temple regime with another. He does not amend the rules of the money-changers and dove-sellers to make them more equitable, or replace them with the more reliable personnel of a more upright temple bureaucracy. Instead of debating the minutiae of temple procedure, Jesus encourages his listeners to focus their minds first on a larger and more glorious vision of the temple's ultimate vocation to be a house of prayer. The detailed questions of how that might be brought about are left for us to determine.

The same refusal of political methods by Jesus might be seen in a unique Matthean detail. Lepers and blind people had been refused access to the temple not only by the law (Leviticus 21:16–20) but also by David himself (2 Samuel 5:8), a key precursor for Jesus here. Yet, in our text Jesus does not admit them to the temple by tearing up or changing the rules – by abrogating a kind of religious-political authority to himself – but by healing them.

The 'humble' kingship of Jesus here achieves its purposes not fundamentally by new legislation, prescription and enforcement, but by articulating with greater clarity the theological vision that should serve as our final goal, and by offering the healing and transformation that enables all to be fully included.

4 The political confrontation

Matthew 27:11–31

Just as Matthew's gospel opens with a confrontation between two kings – Jesus and Herod – so its conclusion begins with a confrontation between Jesus and the highest political authority in the land: Pontius Pilate.

The charge before Pilate is carefully framed. While the earlier trial before the high priest concerns the claim to be 'the Messiah, the Son of God' (Matthew 26:63), here Jesus' opponents misrepresent him in purely political terms, leading Pilate to ask him about the claim to be 'king of the Jews' (v. 11). Jesus' poised silences and indirect answers represent his refusal to be drawn into this political confrontation. They show him rising above a world of political wrangling, of claim and counter-claim, of accusation and self-defence.

The different nature of Jesus' kingship is perhaps most powerfully depicted in the mockery which follows. On one level, the mock coronation is an ironic prophecy simply of the fact that Jesus is a king; the homage of the soldiers reminds the gospel reader of Jesus' kingship, counter to the soldiers' intentions. On a deeper level, however, this cruel encounter is also a revelation of the nature of Jesus' kingship. Counter to our human expectations of political authority and rule, the kingship of Jesus is grounded not in power, or control or revolution, but somehow, mysteriously, in vulnerability, rejection and helplessness. Jesus is not simply a 'good king' to contrast with the 'bad kings' Herod and Pilate, a character who uses political authority to achieve positive change. Rather, his kingship is of a radically different kind, a kind that is revealed not by his ability to impose his will on society, but rather, somehow, by the cruelty with which society imposes its will on him.

This whole passage presents a humbling reversal of our human expectations. We may be seduced by the apparent authority and total control of a Pilate (if only we had his power, we could set the world to rights!). But this encounter reveals that in reality the supposedly powerful political leader is the slave of the crowd. Christ may seem to be the total victim, marginalised, excluded, beaten – but the power of his silences, his disengagement from the political economy of violence and the ceremonies of his bloody coronation indicate that he has indeed overcome the world.

5 The politics of Jesus

John 10:7–21

If the texts we have explored so far complicate our desire to convert Jesus into a political dogma, what can we say about the politics of Jesus?

A starting point might be found in John 10. By describing himself as the good shepherd, Jesus is associating himself with the political rulers of the past. Shepherding was a very popular image for royal rule throughout the ancient Near East. Indeed, David himself is identified as the shepherd who will rule over Israel in Ezekiel 34:23–24.

Yet as soon as he has asserted his claim to the title of shepherd, Jesus immediately emphasises what is unique about his leadership: 'the good shepherd lays down his life for the sheep' (v. 11). Jesus' leadership is wholly grounded in, and to be understood through, his surrender of his life. This is the contrast with the hired hand. The hired hand might be justified in running away; this might be a wise decision, just as political leaders might often have to choose a 'least worst option'. The authority of Jesus the good shepherd is quite different. His leadership authority is grounded not in his pragmatic advocacy of a superior method to minimise harm to the sheep, given the constraints of wolves, but in the fact that he has the authority to lay down his own life and take it up again (v. 18).

This grounding of Jesus' leadership in his death and resurrection has one supreme political consequence. Roman rule was underpinned by an economy of fear. If you did not comply, you might be reprimanded, and if that didn't work, punished, then perhaps beaten, tortured and ultimately killed. While some modern regimes are less brutal, the ability to enforce rules through punitive consequences is a key aspect of all forms of political organisation. Yet, Jesus' willing death and resurrection hope undermine that fear. So for those with faith in Jesus, fear can no longer be the ultimate motivator, nor personal suffering or even death.

While this theological reality does not immediately answer our political questions, it provides us with a horizon to which we can look as we meditate on the social and political challenges that we face in every age. For it demands that we ask ourselves the question: what would my political attitudes be if they were truly formed without fear?

6 Living the politics of Jesus

The parable of the dishonest steward is one of the most hotly debated in the whole of the gospels. For on the surface, it seems to commend a form of dishonesty we find unsettling. It is possible, of course, to read the parable in a less challenging way. The parable is more palatable if we see the point as being: 'those worldly folk are much better at dealing with their crises than we spiritual people are with the impending crisis of judgement – get your act together!' (akin to Luke Timothy Johnson's reading).

Yet such an attempt to clean up the parable underplays both the complexity and the deliberate shock effect of the story. The passage seems to fluctuate between an approbation of canny dealings with money (v. 8) and assertions of the necessity of absolute integrity and probity: 'if, then, you have not been faithful with the dishonest wealth, who will entrust to you the true riches?' (v. 11); 'you cannot serve God and wealth' (v. 13).

For me, at least, this apparent contradiction is creative rather than simply confusing. For it represents the way in which the Christian will inevitably experience the tension between the constant imperatives of goodness and integrity and the need to become entangled in the world's way of doing things in order to achieve the goodness we seek. And this interaction of the need for faithfulness and the need for compromise is the generative tension of Christian moral and political life. To seek to stand completely aloof from this compromised world for the sake of our own purity is as morally reprehensible as to compromise entirely with its practices. For what good can we do if we simply refuse to engage, and what use are we if we completely sell out our principles?

Rather than a manifesto for a new world order, what the readings we have been exploring offer us is a new way of thinking politically. They encourage us to look towards the death and resurrection of Jesus as the horizon and yardstick of all our political thinking as, set free from fear, we seek prayerfully to navigate our way through the necessary complexities and compromises of the life of this world.

Guidelines

If you were hoping to find an election manifesto in these reflections, you may have been disappointed. You will probably have been even more disappointed if you were hoping to find scriptural vindication for any particular set of political views you might hold.

Yet, what I believe these readings place before us is a more devotional and prayerful approach to thinking politically than that to which we are accustomed in our noisy, polemical, polarised and often self-righteous world. Rather than providing a blueprint for our politics, these readings encourage us to ask challenging questions of ourselves about how we think and feel politically, and how compatible our politics truly is with our faith in the death and resurrection of Christ. The following questions might be a place to start our prayerful reflections:

- Have you ever changed your mind about politics/a political issue? What made you do so?

- What are your deepest political convictions? Where do they come from?

- If you can be honest with yourself, how operative is fear in your political thinking?

- Would your politics be the same if Christ had not died and been raised?

- If you can allow yourself to be self-critical, what areas of your political beliefs might you wish to prayerfully rethink?

FURTHER READING

Craig A. Evans, *Matthew (New Cambridge Bible Commentary)* (CUP 2012).

Stanley Hauerwas, *Matthew (SCM Theological Commentary on the Bible)* (SCM Press, 2006).

Luke Timothy Johnson, *The Gospel of Luke (Sacra Pagina)* (The Liturgical Press, 1991).

John Nolland, *Luke 18:35—24:53 (Word Biblical Commentary)* (Thomas Nelson, 1993).

John Howard Yoder, *The Politics of Jesus* (2nd ed., Eerdmans, 1994).

Galatians (part II)

Andrew Boakye

At its heart Galatians has three remarkable high points (2:19; 5:24–25; 6:14–15) depicting the process of being put right in the eyes of God as crucifixion and new existence. In many ways, the letter moves as a crescendo to the third of these high points (the central issue of Gentiles being coerced into circumcision does not even explicitly appear until 5:2). In this final apex, the apostle Paul claims that the world itself has suffered crucifixion and re-emerged as a component of a new creation (6:14–15).

As we shall see, this new creation is governed by a new 'canon' or 'rule' – the canon of Spirit (6:16; compare 5:25). This new canon operates over and against the polarities of the old order, mentioned in 3:28. The specific dichotomy of circumcised–uncircumcised, which is the most pertinent to the rhetoric of Galatians, is explicitly outlined in Galatians 6:15.

Paul's key concern is to demonstrate how the Spirit evokes a revolutionary sensitivity to the divine statutes among believers. The culmination of crucifixion and new life language reflected in Galatians 6 evidences something powerful within Pauline rhetoric. The apostle sees Jesus' body as the canvas of the divine blueprint of salvation. Jesus' body, broken by the effects of sin, represents a world which has suffered a similar fate. Jesus, having been re-embodied through resurrection, symbolises the restoration and reconciliation of the world remade and unshackled by the ravages of sin.

Scholarship on Galatians has slighted the significance of resurrection on the grounds that Jesus' resurrection is only mentioned in the opening line of the letter (and, even then, only as a divine title). However, Galatians demonstrates how the Christ event is the beginning of the fulfilment of the new covenant prophecies and proof of God's covenant faithfulness. God has indeed blessed all nations through Abraham (Genesis 12:3; compare Galatians 3:8) by sending his Spirit to be received through faith (3:14), making one people out of Jew and Gentile (3:26–29) led by the Spirit (5:18) so that love characterises the one people (5:14, 22; 6:2).

Unless otherwise stated, Bible quotations are taken from the NASB.

1 Why then the law?

Galatians 3:16–25

Jewish writers knew Abraham lived prior to the giving of the law, but variously tried to portray him as law-observant – like Philo's claim that Torah simply codified what Abraham did naturally, or the author of *Jubilees* having Abraham observe First Fruits and Tabernacles, festivals instituted by Moses. Paul exploited the historical discrepancy – God's contract with Abraham was not altered by the Torah (v. 17) – if it did, the notion of divine promise to Abraham would be nullified (v. 18).

If God's purposes were met in the Abrahamic covenant, then, as Paul pre-empts in 3:19, why did God give the law? The second half of this verse offers a seemingly plain answer – God *added* the law due to Israel's transgressions until the promised seed, the Messiah (v. 16) appeared. Critical here, however, is *how* the law was given. It was (1) added; (2) through angels; (3) at the hand of a mediator. 'Added' reinforces that the Torah did not supplant God's promise of a son to Abraham and Sarah. 'Through angels' reflects the Jewish tradition that angels accompanied the law-giving (Acts 7:53; Hebrews 2:2; Josephus, *Antiquities* 15.136; Hermas, *Similitudes* 8.3.3). The 'mediator' is Moses (compare Leviticus 26:46).

These three ideas cumulatively point to the *external nature* of the law. Verse 20 appears cryptic, but also points to the law as external entity; 'the mediator is not of one, but God is one' approximates Romans 3:29–30. The mediator is not of one global family; he is a mediator to the one elect family of Israel. However, there is only one God, so a law given to one nation could not ultimately establish right standing before God. God rules over everyone and will justify them on the same basis – *trust*.

If God gave the law to Israel and made the promises to Abraham, are law and promise opposed (v. 21a)? Not a chance – rather, they have two distinct roles. The law's role was to act as 'pedagogue' (v. 24), confining Israel under sin (vv. 22–25) to point Israel to the source of new life; the law itself could not generate life, or else right standing before God would emerge from the law (v. 21b). Once God had brought about new life through Spirit, the law would not be external, but inscribed on the hearts of the people – *this is the new covenant* (see Ezekiel 36:26–27; Jeremiah 31:33; compare 2 Corinthians 3:1–6).

2 Sacred inclusivity

As beautiful a sentence as verse 28 is, it should not be abstracted from its context. Galatians 3:26–29 outlines for the believing community the implications of the relationship between Abraham and Jesus.

The elect people were the seed of Abraham through Isaac. Muslims trace their Abrahamic lineage through Ishmael. Paul argues that the true descendants of Abraham are those who trust in the Messiah. To fully appreciate the passage, we must outline the key idea which indeed links Abraham and the Messiah – *promise*. There is a transitional moment in Galatians 3:14 when the language of promise takes over from the language of blessing:

- 3:14 – the promise is to be identified with the Spirit.

- 3:16 – the promises were spoken to Abraham and his one descendant, the Messiah.

- 3:17 – the law did not disrupt the stipulations of the promise; if it did…

- 3:18 – this would contravene the scriptural notion that God entered a covenant of promise with Abraham – not a legal contract.

- 3:20–21 – the law and the promise have different roles; the promise is the basis of new life.

- 3:22 – the law demonstrates the extent of sin so the promise, the Spirit, might be given to those trusting Messiah (cf. 3:14).

Materially, the promise points to the birth of Isaac, which was 'by the power of the Spirit' (4:28–29). In the birth of Isaac, Abraham experienced the making of miraculous life (compare Romans 4:17–19). The Messiah experienced the same in resurrection. To trust in the risen Messiah, then, is to trust God as Abraham trusted God – trusting in the divine power of revivification. Hence, those who trust in Christ are Abraham's seed according to the promise (v. 29).

Paul equates the descendant of Abraham in verse 29 with sons and daughters of God in verse 26 to demonstrate the juxtaposition with Jesus – *the* Son of God. Trust placed Abraham in right standing before God and correspondingly trust makes believers children of God. In baptism, the believer takes on Messiah, so they also are sons of God as Messiah is *the* Son of God. Trust in the life-making power of God brings believers into the divine family and is why there is no longer any hierarchy of race, gender or social class – only the beautiful oneness of being in Messiah.

3 Spirit: the index of maturity

Galatians 4:1–11

The argument thus far is rehearsed in these verses – this is clarified in the parallel between 3:13–14 and 4:4–6. In both summaries, the Messiah redeems those defined by the law in order that something is received – the Spirit (3:14) and adoption or sonship (v. 5 – note sonship is linked to the Spirit in v. 6).

Having established that the children of Abraham are those 'of Christ' (the singular 'seed' of 3:16) and, therefore, heirs of the promise, Paul outlines a brief family history. While the heirs are children, they are like slaves – they have no inheritance rights (v. 1). They require a chaperone (v. 2) – the Torah – until the specific time set by the Father. This, of course, refers to Israel; in verse 3, Israel (Paul included) was in bondage under the 'elementary principles of the world'. The term translated 'elementary principles' in verses 3 and 9 (Gk. *stoicheia*) typically refers to earth, fire, air and water. Paul defines the law (v. 3) and idols (v. 9) as *stoicheia*. Both cases depict life in the bondage of slavery – Gentiles to idols and Israel under law. Paul is drawing upon the structural integrity that the elements give to the cosmos as a metaphor for enslavement.

The argument is that this bondage evidenced the immaturity of both Israel and the nations – the Spirit himself was the agent by which both Israel and the nations reached maturity and became family. The Bible attests to the Spirit as evidence of the eschatological age (Joel 2:28–32; Isaiah 11:1–10; 44:3); 'in the fullness of time' God sent his Son, to make family from Israel and the nations. As both Jew and Gentile become God's children, Paul calls the Spirit, 'the Spirit of his Son' (compare Romans 8:14–16).

The specific challenge is in verses 8–11; if Gentiles, having been redeemed by trusting Jesus, embrace the Torah (observing days, months and seasons, etc.), it would be to surrender freedom and re-enter slavery.

So there are two, interwoven, controlling metaphors in Galatians – the movements from death to life and from slavery to freedom. This points to Paul's narrative dependence on Ezekiel 37. Both Galatians and Ezekiel describe slavery as death and freedom as life, and this life is a life invoked by the Spirit and leading to a renewed engagement with the laws and decrees of God.

4 Wounds from a friend

Galatians 4:12–20

We all need to hear hard truths sometimes – whether we like it or not – so it is preferable to hear them from a trusted friend: 'Better is open rebuke than hidden love. Well meant are the wounds a friend inflicts, but profuse are the kisses of an enemy' (Proverbs 27:5–6, NRSV).

One can imagine the question in verse 16 being prefaced by, 'You know full-well I love you and would not say anything this caustic unless it was for your good' (compare 2 Corinthians 7:8–9). In Galatians 4:12–20, Paul's rhetoric tugs at the heartstrings to remind the Gentiles of his affection for them, couching any exhortation in love.

Paul reminds the Galatian believers of the illness which originally landed him in Galatia and how they lovingly took him in to help him recover. The comment in verse 15 may point to the illness being eye related – perhaps a lingering effect from a previous beating or perhaps from the Damascus Christophany. Anyway, the Galatians treated Paul as if he were an 'angel of God' or indeed the Messiah himself, and Paul told them of the coming of Israel's Messiah as Lord and Saviour of the world.

However, the infiltrators had shaken their resolve and stolen their joy. Their motives were far from laudable; they were full of zeal, but only to drive a wedge between Paul and the Galatians and make the Galatians zealous for them. They wanted the Galatian Gentiles to feel inferior as Gentiles and elevate their Torah-centred doctrine.

In verses 19–20, one senses Paul's frustration. The very common childbirth metaphor typically denotes the frustrated longing for something to come to fruition, something a woman in labour knows only too well. Paul felt this, longing for the Messiah to be formed in the Galatians. We often read about believers being in Christ, but we cannot slight the notion of Christ being in the believer. Already in 2:19, the apostle has declared that he is alive in a new way quite precisely because 'the Messiah lives in me', and he wants the Galatians to experience the Messiah deep within their consciences and not be hoodwinked by miscreant lectures from pseudo preachers. All the apostle wants is to be with the Galatians face to face and share happier times – for now he must complete this frustrated and defensive warning letter – lest everything be shown to be in vain.

5 Born according to Spirit (1)

Galatians 4:21–26

This closing section of chapter 4 is so dense it will require two parts. The emotional appeal in 4:12–20 serves to introduce 4:21—5:1 which returns to the critical concerns of 3:6–9, where Paul aims to show that faith is the shared gene between God, Abraham and Abraham's children. Where Galatians 3:6–9 employs 'sons of Abraham' as a cypher for God's people, 4:21–31 explicates why God's people are sons of Abraham after the order of Isaac (not Ishmael; compare Romans 9:7). The identification of Isaac as the son of promise illustrates how he is the precursor and progenitor of those who trust in Messiah.

The apostle longs for these Galatian Gentiles to experience true formation; but wanting to be under law shows they have not comprehended it (v. 21); the law cannot produce life (3:21) so is not the grounds of the covenant with Abraham (3:17–18). Paul is about to hint at why.

The promise made to Abraham (Genesis 15:6) was to have a son with his wife against all embryological odds. Given Abraham and Sarah's age, conceiving was impossible without divine intervention – so Isaac was not born through the usual channels of biological probability, *but because God promised*. 'Life' was produced in the form of Isaac's birth because of the power of the God who, through his Spirit, makes life (recall Genesis 2:7). This narrative, explicit in Romans 4:16–25, is embedded in Galatians 4:21—5:1.

According to the law, Abraham had a child by a slave woman (Hagar) and a child by Sarah, who is free (v. 22). Hagar's child was born according to the flesh – through ordinary biological channels. Sarah's child was born *through promise* (Greek, *dia epangēlias*) because the natural conditions did not favour conception (v. 23). Paul reasons that Hagar and Sarah represent the Mount Sinai covenant and the Abrahamic covenant respectively. Hagar, being a slave, will only give birth to slave children – prefiguring those enslaved by the Torah (4:24–25a; recall 4:1–7). They are tied to the Jerusalem of the present age, *a city under Roman rule* (4:25b). The eschatological people of God are tied to the Jerusalem above, the Jerusalem of the new age, which is free and represents the finality of God's purposes (compare Hebrews 12:22; Revelation 21:2). The Jerusalem above is 'our mother' for she gives birth to the children of freedom corresponding to Isaac – who trust in the Messiah.

6 Born according to Spirit (2)

Paul then attempts to undergird his argument by citing Isaiah 54:1 (NRSV):
*Shout for joy, O barren one who has borne no children; burst into song
and shout, you who have not been in labour! For the children of the deso-
late woman will be more than the children of the one who is married,
says the Lord.*

It is the principle and not the detail that Paul wishes to employ here; the
correspondence is not direct because in Genesis, the barren woman *is* the
married woman, Sarah. However, the principle is plain for readers of Isaiah.
In Isaiah 26:17–19, rebellious Israel enslaved in Assyria is a pregnant woman
giving birth to air. Those who would eventually be freed are described as
corpses raised from the dead. In Isaiah 54, the prophet's attentions have
turned to Judah in slavery in Babylon, depicted using another death metaphor – barrenness – so the freedom of new life is represented by childbirth.
These metaphors are pivotal to the story of Abraham, Sarah and Hagar. The
barren Sarah gives life to Isaac who is free (note again the connection between
resurrection and freedom as in Ezekiel 37). It is in the remaining verses of the
section that Paul delivers the killer blows.

Galatians 4:28: Paul declares that Galatian Gentiles are children of the
promise according to Isaac, by God's grace, through trust in Messiah.

Galatians 4:29: the apostle here makes the same equation we have seen
earlier in the chapter: birth according to promise is birth according to Spirit
(compare 3:14). For Isaac to be born according to the Spirit means he was
brought to life because God decreed he would live, despite the overwhelming odds of Abraham and Sarah conceiving at their age; Isaac's birth was
a resurrection miracle (compare Romans 4:16–25). To be justified through
trusting Jesus is ontologically a movement from death to life, so Isaac's birth
foreshadows justification. Justification is how those who trust Jesus become
true sons of Abraham.

Galatians 4:30–31: the troublemakers should be expelled from the Galatian
Jesus community!

The first verse of chapter 5 is likely a summation of the argument from
4:21. Those trusting in Messiah were freed by him – to embrace Jewish cultic
practice would be to give up one's freedom and be re-enslaved. It is now that
Paul outlines the rival teachers' agenda – calling for Gentile circumcision.

11–17 November   87

Guidelines

The law of Moses was given specifically to the Israelites, newly freed from captivity in Egypt, to keep their sin in check until such time that the Messiah, the ultimate antidote for sin, appeared on the scene (3:19–25). No law given to one ethnic group could be the final word on what it meant to be in right relationship with God, for there is but one God, and Moses only had jurisdiction over Israel (3:20; compare Romans 3:29–30). To truly be in right relationship with God meant to be revivified with the life of the new age; but the law was never imbued with the capacity to revivify (3:21).

The Mosaic law pointed to the Messiah (3:24). In the Messiah, both Jew and Gentile enter a new mode of existence through the Spirit. To be born according to the Spirit, as Isaac was born, is to enter this new mode of existence energised by the risen life of Jesus (4:28–29; compare Romans 4:16–25). This is the life of the new age (1:4), and the dawn of a new kind of maturity (4:1–11) where, on the basis of the Spirit, God's people will have a renewed proclivity to engage with his commands.

The Spirit ended Israel's enslavement under the law in the same way that the Spirit ended the nations' enslavement under idolatry (4:4–9). How do freedom and maturity relate to one another? In what ways do younger believers need shepherding and stewarding that older believers do not? How ought we think about the tutelage of new believers so that they develop maturity and a Spirit-led affinity to be God-reliant and not people-reliant?

How do we encourage the ability to have difficult conversations in Christian fellowship? How do we avoid 'becoming one another's enemies by telling the truth'? When was the last time you needed to have a very difficult conversation with someone? How did you approach it? On reflection, are there things you might have done differently?

1 When faith works through love

Galatians 5:2–12

After the Maccabean resistance, Jews sought to reinforce markers of Jewish identity and especially circumcision. Some Jews, acquiescing to pressure to embrace Greek ideas, attempted to reverse their circumcisions by a process called epispasm (see 1 Maccabees 1:15). Certain Jews even embarked on a campaign of forced circumcision on some of their captives. For zealous Jews, circumcision became a litmus test for authenticity. In the book of *Jubilees*, angels were circumcised at creation (*Jubilees* 15.11–14). The Essenes believed the uncircumcised would be destroyed in the judgement.

In light of the above, it is unsurprising that Jewish sects not demanding circumcision might be perceived as compromisers. The Christian Pharisees in Acts 15:5 were adamant that Gentile believers embraced circumcision. Paul was adamant they did not!

In Galatians 6:14–15, the Christ event split the world into two ages; in the age of the Spirit, polarities like circumcised/uncircumcised are effectively eradicated. As such, to undergo circumcision obliged someone to the entire law – a law which cannot produce the life of the new age (3:21). Hence, undergoing circumcision cut one off from the Messiah (5:4). The apostle is not celebrating uncircumcision over circumcision, but relativising both in view of Messiah – what matters is, in the context of Christ's love, faith brings right relationship with God (5:5–6). Indeed, verse 11 may suggest that Paul himself once preached circumcision. However, Paul now preaches the cross, as the persecution against him proves.

Paul's rage here is reminiscent of the meal table drama in Antioch (Galatians 2). Embracing circumcision or Kashrut was, for Paul, like suggesting the inadequacy of Jesus' sacrifice to accomplish God's purposes. If justification required trust in Christ *plus* Jewish ethnicity, then the gospel had failed to launch. Being in right relationship with God was the process of crucifixion and new life (2:19; 5:24–25), transforming people into God's children, precisely because *the* Son of God had experienced literal crucifixion and resurrection. Anyone in Christ has been revivified, entering the divine family and living the life of the new age, irrespective of ethnicity. To reintroduce ethno-specificity by insisting on circumcision is to undermine the world-embracing work of God.

2 Love fulfils the law

Galatians 5:13–26

An early 2nd-century Christian manual known as the *Didache* opens with the following charge:

> *There are two ways, one of life and one of death… The way of life is this. First of all, thou shalt love the God that made thee; secondly, thy neighbour as thyself. And all things whatsoever thou would not have befall thyself, neither do thou unto another.*

A Gentile seeking to embrace Torah asked the Pharisee Shammai to teach him the whole law. Shammai shooed him away; Rabbi Hillel told him, 'What is hateful to you, do not do to your neighbour; that is the whole Torah, while the rest is the commentary thereof' (compare Mark 12:29–31).

For Jews like Paul, commitment to the Torah was summed up in the golden rule (Leviticus 19:18). With the Galatian Jesus community divided between those loyal to Paul's gospel and those enticed by his rivals, Paul felt impelled to remind his listeners where the law pointed all along – love.

The apostle's teaching outlines how the law is fulfilled in an awkward paradox. To trust in the Messiah is to embrace a unique freedom – freedom to be mutually enslaved to one another with love, not law, as master. A pivotal element of the new covenant prophecies taking shape amidst the Galatian believers was how this love, which summed up the Torah, would be accomplished by the Spirit. Without the Spirit's intervention, the community would succumb to the vices outlined in verses 19–21, eight of which are directly related to disunity and the breakdown of community cohesion (hostilities, strife, jealousy, angry outbursts, selfish ambition, dissensions and factions). These vices evidence the weak, fragile and susceptible component of the human condition, flesh, and are opposed to the Spirit.

If, however, the community was not beholden to the written law, some might wonder how community ethics were established. Verse 18 says plainly – ethics came from the Spirit-led proclivity to engage with God's commands in profoundly new fashion. The Spirit did not offer a new set of rules but a new mode of existence, evidenced by the virtues listed in 5:22–23, headed by love, and against which there was no 'law'.

One might sum up the new covenant thus – the law, internalised in the heart under the auspices of the Spirit, generates a community-forming, family-enhancing, mutually enslaving love.

3 The law of Messiah

It seems from Galatians 5:10 that the ringleader of the rival teachers is unknown to the community – yet the community is split. Paul's wording implies no one had actually succumbed to circumcision, but a schism was forming; some were persuaded by the infiltrators' rhetoric. After all, Abraham was commanded to circumcise all his children as a sign of the covenant (Genesis 17). Sabbath observance was one of the ten commandments (Exodus 20:8). Gentiles had to abandon idolatry and sexual misconduct (Acts 15:20). Adding Kosher regulations to this list was scarcely a stretch.

Nonetheless, Paul was unflinching; to insist on observing Jewish cultural markers meant devaluing Christ-faith and making justification ethno-specific. Anyone lulled into thinking in this way needed correcting.

Those 'of the Spirit' were to responsibly help the ones hoodwinked by the false teaching. Paul describes bearing one another's burdens as completely fulfilling the law of Messiah, mirroring the statement in 5:14, wherein mutual enslavement in the context of love fulfils Leviticus 19:18. The connection seems clear; the Messiah is the ultimate burden-bearer, expressed in his enslavement to those he loves. As Mark notes, the Son of Man came not to be served but to serve and to give his life as a ransom for many (Mark 10:45). Life led by the Spirit is not a life under the law but with the law internalised. Those who have been set free by their trust in Messiah have the Spirit of Messiah and are sons (Galatians 4:6), as foretold by Ezekiel – God would put his Spirit in the people and change their hearts from stone to flesh (Ezekiel 36:26). As Jeremiah predicted, divine law would be inscribed on people's hearts (Jeremiah 31:33). The Spirit-kindled internalisation of the divine law and the divinely inspired renewal of sensitivity to the divine law is the law of the Messiah.

Hence, the apostle commands those 'spiritual ones' (Gk. *hoi pneumatikoi*) to restore the wayward; these are the ones who have internalised the Torah under the auspices of the Spirit, and by gently restoring those caught in the trespass of following the false gospel demonstrate that they are enslaved to them in mutual love.

To a related question, this tells us what kind of Jew Paul was: he was a new covenant resurrectionist. Paul understood the eschatology of restoration from exile taking shape within new communities formed around the resurrection of Messiah.

4 Sowing to the Spirit

Galatians 6:3–8

There is a very significant eschatological clarification that Paul must add here. Although bearing one another's burdens fulfils the law of Messiah (v. 2), each one will carry his own load (v. 5). The change to the future tense points to the one burden no one else can carry for you – the eschatological reckoning at the judgement. When it comes to the judgement, although it is right to be grateful for those who have helped you along the way (v. 6), each person will have to examine themselves and the life they have lived (v. 4). About this there can be no confusion – God will certainly not be under any delusions (v. 7) – those who indulge the flesh will reap destruction. Those who sow to the Spirit – again, we ought to think of those spiritual ones, alive by the Spirit on the basis of trusting Messiah – will inherit the life of the new age. As such, Paul urges the community to continue in love and good deeds, especially towards one another – and in view of his previous instruction, this probably goes double towards those led astray by the rival preachers' phoney gospel.

The metaphor of reaping what one sows is common in both ancient religious and secular literature. When Paul uses the metaphor, it is quite likely he has been ruminating on Psalm 126, where sowing and reaping involved a difficult choice. In Psalm 126:5, sowing in tears likely reflects the painful choice of a farmer during a famine or a drought – should he use the seed to feed his family now or sow the seed for a harvest later? The next verse is an assurance that even making the harder decision to sow will pay off if the psalmist will only trust.

Paul is consistent with his use of the word 'flesh' in Galatians. Contextually, it points once more to those external markers of identity. To invest in these is to deny the internalisation of the Spirit. It is in this that God is not mocked; those who identify with the external markers of identity in this life will not enter the renewed life marked by the Spirit in the age to come. To sow to the Spirit is to identify with the crucified and risen Christ; this is the more painful choice, but greater benefits are to be reaped.

5 Cosmos crucified, cosmos renewed (1)

Believing Jews were under fire as more Gentiles joined the Galatian Jesus community. Jewish people enjoyed exemptions from the imperial cult and local idol-feasts as a concession from Rome; as the Romans did not distinguish between Jewish sects, these exemptions were extended to the Jesus movement. Of course, all Gentiles were expected to participate in the local festivals and the imperial cultus. However, as Gentiles joined the Jesus movement, they gradually rejected the 'gods'. The exemptions given to Jews did not extend to Gentiles – even Christ-believing Gentiles – and this created conflict. For Rome, excusing the Jews from idolatry was an act of political expediency, and they expected Jewish support in reciprocal exchange for this pardon. If Gentile Christ-believers started expecting the same pardon, the entire exchange might be jeopardised. Hence, the synagogue resented Jewish Christ-believers who did not demand that Gentiles embrace Jewish cultic practice.

Verses 12–13, then, are Paul's appraisal of the strategy of some Jewish believers – if they could compel Gentiles to be circumcised and be seen as Jews, they would avoid persecution and look good to the synagogue – they could 'boast in your flesh' (brag to the Jews that they had circumcised Gentiles).

Paul, far from a boast which *bypassed* the cross, would boast only in *the cross itself.* The apostle took particular exception to boasting – see 1 Corinthians 1:31 (citing Jeremiah 9:24) and Romans 3:27. However, it is Paul's reason for boasting in the cross which illuminates this section of the argument.

A theme running through Galatians is that crucifixion stands for a destruction which pre-empts new life. Of the four references to 'crucify' in the letter, only 3:1 refers to Jesus. In 2:19, Paul suffers crucifixion to live the new life 'to God'. In 5:24–25, the Gentiles suffer crucifixion and live according to the Spirit. In verses 14 Paul revisits his co-crucifixion, adding that he has been crucified to the cosmos and, indeed, the cosmos has itself suffered crucifixion. Messiah has imbued the believers with the identity-transforming energy of resurrection and has done so for the cosmos. The death of Jesus was a cosmic fissure which divided the universe into two distinct aeons, as argued by J. Louis Martyn in his commentary on Galatians (see further reading list). The majority scholarly position held that the second coming of Jesus divided the world into ages. The reading offered here corroborates Martyn's position, but for that we need another session.

6 Cosmos crucified, cosmos renewed (2)

Galatians 6:15–18

The crucified cosmos meant the complete disruption of the hierarchical polarities which burdened the old order, limiting its flourishing, causing friction between people groups and promoting hatred, discord and superiority. So, Paul concludes, within the renewed cosmos, emerging from the old order, the distinction circumcised versus uncircumcised carries no weight. What matters is the new creation, freed from these distinctions and where people can be truly free.

The benediction in verse 16 is pronounced on all who walk according to this new 'canon'. The verb usually translated 'walk' is used in 5:25 – Gentiles, alive by Spirit, must 'walk' by Spirit (the only other use of the verb in Galatians). The inference is that the 'canon' or 'rule' of verse 16 is the canon of the Spirit and corresponds to the other imperatives connected to a Spirit imbued life – walking in (5:16), being led by (5:18), exhibiting the fruits of (5:22) and sowing to (6:8) the Spirit. It is unclear, though, whether those walking according to Spirit and Paul's 'Israel of God' are the same group or two different ones. Is Paul pronouncing peace on those who walk according to the canon of Spirit and mercy upon the Israel of God, or 'peace and mercy upon the Israel of God' – defined as those who walk according to the canon of Spirit? The contextual contours of the epistle suggest the latter – the Israel of God represents the multi-ethnic family of God defined by the Spirit, not the Torah.

These closing ideas are not a mere addendum; they were significant enough for Paul to take the pen from his amanuensis (secretary) and write them himself with his characteristic handwriting (6:11; compare 2 Thessalonians 3:17; Romans 16:22). These closing thoughts effectively conclude and summarise the entire epistle. Paul includes a somewhat cynical note that those outside the Israel of God (probably the rogue teachers) should not cause him further trouble, for he bears on his body the marks (literally the 'stigmata') of proclaiming Jesus and his cross. Western readers are unlikely to ever bear the physical marks of persecution for the cross in their bodies, but non-western readers may, and should take encouragement from Paul's words. However, in whatever way the marks of Messiah, visible or otherwise, are inflicted on us for his sake, we also ought to bear them, taking encouragement from Galatians and Paul's own commitment to the Messiah.

Guidelines

If the law was given to point to the Messiah, what would the ethical barometer of the community be? Paul has one answer – the Spirit. The Spirit of God would make the commands and statutes of God an inner, spiritual reality (6:1–2; compare 5:24–25). This is what lies at the heart of the new covenant, which, for Paul, was taking shape because the death and resurrection of Jesus had altered the very fabric of the cosmos (6:14). The old world had suffered crucifixion and re-emerged as part of a new creation, also energised by the resurrection energy of the Messiah (6:14–15). Within the realms of this new creation, the polarities which burdened the old order like circumcised versus uncircumcised, male versus female, slave versus free (6:15; compare 3:28), were expunged of their capacity to create hierarchy. The Spirit, who dwelt in God's people through trust in Messiah, made them one people, without hierarchy and newly awakened to what it meant to live in unified community with love at the centre (5:13–14) but without the need for the written law (5:16–25).

- Think through the ways in which hierarchy and domination have historically damaged societies. How can the church offer a countercultural vision of community?

- What are the challenges involved in unifying Christian communities? What sort of things divide believing communities?

- How does the resurrection of Jesus help us to think about the nature of change both within and outside the community? In what ways does reflecting on Galatians help us evaluate and wrestle with resurrection?

FURTHER READING

John Barclay, *Paul and the Power of Grace* (Eerdmans, 2020).

Andrew Boakye, *Death and Life: Resurrection, restoration and rectification in Paul's letter to the Galatians* (Pickwick Publications, 2017).

Neil Martin, *Galatians Reconsidered: Jews, Gentiles and justification in the first and the twenty-first centuries* (Apollos, 2022).

Peter Oakes and Andrew Boakye, *Rethinking Galatians: Paul's vision of oneness in the living Christ* (T&T Clark, 2021).

Jarvis J. Williams, *The Spirit, Ethics, and Eternal Life: Paul's vision for the Christian life in Galatians* (Inter Varsity Press, 2023).

N.T. Wright, *Galatians* (Eerdmans, 2021).

Prayers in the New Testament

Olivia Warburton

Even restricting my focus to the gospels and Acts, it was a challenging exercise to select only six prayers for this set of notes! I concentrated on prayer in action: people praying in the moment; direct speech, rather than reports of prayer taking place.

What can we learn from these brief tableaux? As always with more thematic studies, the criticism can be that they feel bitty, disjointed, maybe even biased towards a particular writer's pet enthusiasm. But as part of a healthy diet of more sustained narrative exposition, the more lateral approach can and should enlighten us and enable us to make connections across the Bible, or within a particular book, that one might miss in digesting more meaty chunks of text. As C.S. Lewis would say, albeit in a different context, 'Looking along the beam and looking at the beam are very different experiences. You get one experience of a thing when you look along it and another when you look at it' ('Meditation in a Toolshed', originally published in *The Coventry Evening Telegraph* on 17 July 1945). Both have much to offer.

Looking 'along' the theme of prayer, therefore, the first thing to note is just how many examples of prayer there are in the gospels and Acts, not to mention how frequently Paul and the other New Testament writers pray in their epistles. It's a truism nevertheless worth highlighting, because we can then start to explore the different types of prayer – and the different types of pray-er – and the situations in which prayer is happening. Prayer in public, prayer in private, with friends, with strangers, as part of worship. By Jew, by Gentile, for oneself, for others. For healing, for relief, for rescue, for guidance, for blessing, as thanksgiving. I hope that this slender offering will whet your appetite to examine the many other examples that lie within the biblical text and, most importantly, to consider how these can inform our own individual and corporate experiences of prayer.

Bible quotations are taken from the NIV.

1 I have every confidence

Matthew 8:5–13

Let's start with a prayer that takes even Jesus by surprise. It's one of the key moments in the gospels where Jesus is taken aback by the faith of someone who isn't even part of the people of Israel (see also the Canaanite woman in Matthew 15:21–28). In a sad inversion, he is also amazed by the lack of faith of his own townspeople in Galilee, with the result that 'he could not do any miracles there' (Mark 6:5–6).

The centurion's prayer is a prayer for help, specifically for healing, and not for himself but for a servant. It is remarkable that the centurion cares so much for a servant to go to the trouble of seeking Jesus out. His compassion is also indicated in the detail he gives that the man is paralysed and 'suffering terribly' (v. 6). Jesus' question to him, 'Shall I come and heal him?', suggests that the centurion has not in his request specified what he wants Jesus to do. In prayer, perhaps we do not always need to outline the desired solution, but rather present our petition to God trusting that he will know the best outcome better than we could ourselves.

The second remarkable aspect of the centurion's prayer is a humility that actually pushes back against Jesus' proffered grace: 'I do not deserve to have you come under my roof' (v. 8). There is an echo here of other people of faith who dared to negotiate the divine status quo, secure in what they understood of the divine character (for example, Abraham pleading for a reprieve for Sodom in Genesis 18; the Canaanite woman making her case for inclusion in Matthew 15). Clearly the centurion recognises his sinfulness in comparison with the holiness of the Saviour. But he has another reason for waiving the offer: he has absolute confidence that Jesus doesn't actually need to come; that complete and immediate healing, at a distance, is well within Jesus' power to bestow. His understanding of military authority and hierarchy translates instinctively into a grasp of the spiritual authority that Jesus holds over all other powers and authorities, including sickness and death itself. No wonder Jesus is amazed.

Lord Jesus, help me to come before you with humble confidence in your saving power. Amen.

2 Prayer as a group effort

Mark 7:31–37

We all know that we can't outsource our faith lives, relying on our religious background, family or church community to make us right with God. So what is going on here? Isn't this prayer by proxy? There is no indication in the narrative that the man in question has prayed, or has even come to Jesus of his own accord. He does nothing; can barely talk and cannot hear. His friends bring him and 'beg' Jesus to heal him (v. 32).

These friends, like those who brought the paralysed man to Jesus and lowered him through the roof (Mark 2:1–12; Luke 5:17–26), are clearly friends in need and friends indeed, although their garrulous response to the miracle, while understandable, is not what Jesus had wanted. (An unresolved question is whether the man himself, once able to speak, is similarly garrulous; it is possible to read the text as referring to the crowd/friends while the man himself, perhaps wiser, holds his counsel.)

But Jesus is, it seems, primarily concerned with the man himself: taking him away from the crowd (and one assumes those very friends) to a quiet place where he can tune in without distractions to the man's situation. At other times, as at the pool of Bethesda, he asks the sufferer, 'Do you want to get well?' (John 5:6) or, to blind Bartimaeus, 'What do you want me to do for you?' (Mark 10:51). But here the man cannot communicate; the assumption is, therefore, that Jesus sees his heart and his wish to be healed and grants the unspoken prayer. Perhaps this is similar to what Paul later describes as the Spirit helping us in our weakness: 'The Spirit himself intercedes for us through wordless groans' (Romans 8:26), or, as the RSV puts it, 'sighs too deep for words'. There is a linguistic reflection of this in verse 34, where Jesus 'looked up to heaven and with a deep sigh said to him, "Ephphatha!" (which means "Be opened!")'. The suggestion is that Jesus is praying to his Father in heaven, interceding for the man.

It is indeed a group effort: friends, suffering man, Jesus himself, all engaging in prayer which is not necessarily spoken. And it is encouragement that even incapacitation and disability cannot stand in the way of the soul's quest for Jesus, who sees the desires of our hearts.

Amazing grace! Lord Jesus, we praise your creative mercy to bring about restoration where none seems possible. Amen.

3 How not to pray

Luke 18:9-14

In Matthew 6:9-13 Jesus gives his disciples a template for prayer, one which combines intimate trust in God as our Father with appropriate reverence for the creator of the universe. To a different audience, he moves from template to parable, contrasting two types of prayer with a pointed take-home message for those whose 'prayers' were in reality nothing of the sort. The Pharisee in the story is arguably a caricature. Would even the most self-righteous individual stand in the temple and give voice to these sentiments – even if he privately thought them? More likely, if this were a cartoon, we'd see these words in a thought bubble. Jesus is exaggerating to make a point, and it's one all of us can take to heart, for we have all been quietly self-satisfied at times, and comparisons are easy and comforting to make. Jesus wanted anyone who was 'confident of their own righteousness and looked down on everyone else' (v. 9) to realise that exalting themselves was not the route to honest relationship with God. As he says at the start of the chapter where the Lord's Prayer appears, in relation to giving, 'Be careful not to practise your righteousness in front of others to be seen by them' (Matthew 6:1).

The Pharisee stands in contrast to the centurion of Matthew 8, who we have already looked at. Jesus' invented tax collector (perhaps based on the real-life Zacchaeus/Matthew), like the centurion, recognises the gulf between himself, as a flawed human being, and the almighty God. Given his profession, he would have been understood by Jesus' audience to have some glaring offences of which to repent. Yet rather than cataloguing his failings as the Pharisee catalogues his merits, the tax collector's prayer is breathtaking in its simplicity. He offers no defence, and none is needed.

This prayer, like the Lord's Prayer, has been prayed through the ages and across traditions, adapted slightly to become what is known as the Jesus Prayer. Hidden in this parable, another of Jesus' template prayers can be found.

Lord Jesus Christ, Son of God, have mercy on me, a sinner.

4 Prayer unpacked

In John's gospel, prayer goes public. In the synoptic gospels, Jesus typically prays alone, and he instructs his followers to pray in private: 'When you pray, go into your room, close the door and pray to your Father, who is unseen' (Matthew 6:6). He also discourages lengthy prayers: 'Do not keep on babbling like pagans, for they think they will be heard because of their many words. Do not be like them, for your Father knows what you need before you ask him' (vv. 7–8).

Turning to John's gospel, we see a somewhat different approach. We do not see Jesus teaching about prayer, for example. We also see a more public, even performative, approach to prayer, notably at the raising of Lazarus (John 11:41–42). In John 17, Jesus' prayer is also in the presence of others, albeit a small group of trusted friends; and the brevity advocated in the other gospels is absent.

Contradictory? John's gospel is the odd one out in many ways, and his rendering of Jesus' prayer at that final meal is consistent with his habit of identifying key themes within his wider narrative and drawing them out at length. John wants to hammer home certain messages, and here he fully unwraps the Easter eggs hidden earlier in his gospel: John's desire is for Christ's glory to be revealed and for all to understand the love between Father and Son, the love of Jesus for his disciples both at that time and far into the future, and the love all disciples of Christ are commanded to have for each other.

In order to achieve his aim, it is arguable that John is unpacking and amplifying Jesus' possibly much briefer original prayer, or synthesising words and ideas communicated at different times during Jesus' ministry. Thus this prayer, with its sense of formality and gravitas, whether inherent or bestowed, has come to be dignified by special labels: the Farewell Prayer, the High Priestly Prayer, the Prayer for Unity or even the 'real' Lord's Prayer. In the disciple whom Jesus loved, we sense a creative, expansive, poetic attitude to prayer. Jesus' prayer for unity of purpose did not, after all, exclude diversity of expression.

Lord Jesus, may the theme of my prayers, like yours, be love and glory, unity and blessing, however I may be led to express them. Amen.

5 The rule of three

Matthew 26:36–46

The rule of three is a centuries-old communication principle: that things which come in threes are inherently more satisfying, effective and memorable. Its effectiveness is attributed to the fact that three is the smallest number of pieces needed to make a pattern. Here Jesus prays a prayer of renunciation, 'Yet not as I will, but as you will' (v. 39), and he prays 'the same thing' (v. 44) three times. A little later, in the high priest's courtyard, Peter denies Jesus three times (vv. 69–75), growing increasingly categorical until the cock crows. Peter's repeated denial is surely intended to contrast painfully with Jesus' virtuous repetition; Jesus triumphs in the moment of testing as Peter fails. We find Peter's restoration in John 21:15–19, again in the rule of three as Jesus instructs him three times to 'feed my sheep'.

We've seen in the healing story in Mark 7 how Jesus collaborates with his heavenly Father and with others in prayer. Here, however, the group fails him and he is alone. His disciples cannot stay awake – not once, but twice. If there is dialogue with his heavenly Father, it is not shared: the impression is one of silence, of words cast into the void, as when later Jesus hangs on the cross, crying, 'My God, my God, why have you forsaken me?' (Matthew 27:46). This is prayer that holds on by its fingertips; all it can do is to repeat itself until some kind of completeness is achieved by virtue of attaining the third time of asking. Jesus is 'sorrowful and troubled… overwhelmed… to the point of death' (vv. 37–38). His comment to Peter, 'Watch and pray so that you will not fall into temptation. The spirit is willing, but the flesh is weak,' is also an exhortation to himself, utterly committed to the salvation path that lies before him but recoiling instinctively from what it will involve.

All of this is foreshadowed in Matthew 6:9–13, where Jesus taught his disciples to pray. Now in the garden he prays, 'Your will be done' (v. 10), and his words to Peter echo verse 13: 'And lead us not into temptation, but deliver us from the evil one.' Here, Jesus is practising what he preached, once, twice and three times, until the pattern is established and he is able to face what lies ahead.

Lord Jesus, may I be enabled to pray as you did, over and over if need be, until the point of resolution. Amen.

6 Even when you're not doing it right

Here's further encouragement! Cornelius is praying to the God of Israel, but he isn't a Christian. Still, he's committed and disciplined, and prays regularly and seriously. Not only that, but he puts his money where his mouth is. An angel tells him, 'Your prayers and gifts to the poor have come up as a memorial offering before God' (v. 5); and since offerings are sacrificial, it would seem that Cornelius is giving over and above what might be expected, and possibly more than he could comfortably afford. His devotion has certainly been sufficient to gain him a special angelic visitation and, furthermore, a special encounter with the apostle Peter. Note the difference from the Pharisee in Jesus' parable in Luke 18 – Cornelius is not shown as boasting of his donations.

Cornelius is in the act of prayer at three in the afternoon when he has the vision of the angel (v. 3), just as Peter's vision comes during a time of prayer the following day (v. 9). As with so many of the biblical characters who are visited by angels, Cornelius is afraid; but he is immediately reverent ('Lord') while also being commendably direct ('What is it?') to the point of bluntness (v. 4). Like the centurion in Matthew 8, Cornelius knows how to obey orders to the letter, and he proceeds to carry out the angel's instructions without question or delay.

We don't know anything of the content of Cornelius' prayers: praise? thanksgiving? intercession? confession? The key thing appears to be that they were regular, a clear sign of his commitment, as his Roman background in no way mandated this routine of prayer in terms of cultural expectations. Regular prayer was Cornelius' free choice. The other significant element of his prayer was its outflowing into generous, sacrificial giving; prayer and giving are two parts of the whole, combining into the 'memorial offering' which so pleased God.

Without any comment on Cornelius's theological shortcomings, God sent his angel to help the centurion towards fuller understanding. For Cornelius, simply doing what he felt to be right, faithfully and sincerely, with far-from-complete revelation of God's saving plan in Jesus Christ, was acceptable to God and honoured by him.

Lord Jesus, may we accept and encourage each other at all stages on our journeys of life and faith. Amen.

Guidelines

As we reflect on these scriptures, there's plenty here to inform our own prayers. The following questions provide prompts drawn from each of the six passages we've looked at.

- Reflect on the centurion's striking combination of confidence and humility.
- How could we harness the power of praying together in our communities to achieve God's purposes?
- How do I pray… really?
- How can we celebrate, and experiment with, diverse ways of praying?
- How can I make sure that I pray and keep on praying?
- Am I open to God working in the least likely people, and truly accepting of them?

In the following poem, George Herbert provides numerous synonyms for prayer. Which idea speaks most helpfully to you, and why?

Prayer the church's banquet, angel's age,
God's breath in man returning to his birth,
The soul in paraphrase, heart in pilgrimage,
The Christian plummet sounding heav'n and earth.
Engine against th' Almighty, sinner's tow'r,
Reversed thunder, Christ-side-piercing spear,
The six-days world transposing in an hour,
A kind of tune, which all things hear and fear;
Softness, and peace, and joy, and love, and bliss,
Exalted manna, gladness of the best,
Heaven in ordinary, man well drest,
The milky way, the bird of Paradise,
Church-bells beyond the stars heard, the soul's blood,
The land of spices; something understood.

George Herbert (1593–1633)

Forgiveness

David Spriggs

'Forgiveness' is one of the central concerns and core concepts of the Christian faith. The Lord's Prayer contains the memorable and challenging lines, 'And forgive us our debts, as we also have forgiven our debtors' (Matthew 6:12, compare verse 14). A claim of Jesus which greatly troubled the religious leaders was: '"But so that you may know the Son of Man has authority on earth to forgive sins" – he said to the paralytic – "I say to you, stand up…"' (Mark 2:10–11). The amazing prayer from the cross is, 'Father, forgive them, for they do not know what they are doing' (Luke 23:34).

Forgiveness is not as simple a concept as we might imagine. The dictionary definition is 'to cease to feel resentment against', 'to grant pardon for', 'to give up all claim on account of (a debt)' and we need to be careful not to import connotations when the texts are in Hebrew or Greek. For instance, in Matthew's version of the Lord's Prayer 'forgiveness' is situated in a financial context, the implication being that 'forgiveness' requires the cancellation of any debt. Whilst this does not restrict the meaning to financial transactions, it provides a nuance. So, we will best understand forgiveness in connection with various related concepts such as guilt, punishment, remission, ransom, pardon and the nature of sin and ultimately God himself. We also need to keep our eye on issues such as the dynamics of forgiveness (God – human; human – human) and the subject – individuals, collective or national.

Unless otherwise stated, Bible quotations are from the NRSV.

1 The big picture

Genesis 3:1–24

The context for much Christian thinking about forgiveness is provided by this passage. Not all those writing about forgiveness in the Old Testament would necessarily have this in their minds. Equally, it is primarily Paul in the New Testament who carries consciousness of this setting, although clearly Jesus was aware of and engaged with the early part of Genesis.

What, then, does this chapter contribute to our understanding of forgiveness? On a superficial reading, not a lot, because 'forgiveness' is not mentioned, and it concludes with a passage which appears to be the opposite of forgiveness. The man and woman are driven from the garden of Eden and prevented from ever returning. Yet this is not the whole story.

We are given insight as to why forgiveness is required. Verses 1–8 reveal three core things. While the heart of the problem is that of disobedience to God's commandment, within this there are several layers. First, doubting that God's intentions towards us are always and completely good (vv. 3–5). Second, doubting the reality of the consequences of disobeying God – 'You will not die' (v. 4). And third, listening to other voices and giving them priority over God's.

We also discover two other important aspects of sin. First, that many of our senses can be involved in the allure of it – survival (good food), aesthetic satisfaction ('a delight to the eyes'), intellectual competence ('to make one wise'). Second, that sin is more than a personal choice – Eve is influenced by the serpent and Adam by his wife.

But the dominant factor is that sin divides us – from one another, and above all from God. How futile and sad that Adam and Eve should think they can hide from God, and even more significantly that they now feel the need to hide from God.

The rest of the chapter shows God holding Adam and Eve to account, leading to some kind of confession (vv. 8–13), and God's words to the serpent, the woman and the man (vv. 14–19) where appropriate consequences are decreed, indicating that the consequences of sin are proportionate and apposite. However, we should not miss verse 21, where God 'made garments of skin… and clothed them'. Their futile 'fig leaves' are replaced by God's adequate, gracious and merciful provision.

2 The sin-offering

Leviticus 4:1–2, 13–21, 27–31; 5:11–13

How God would continue his adequate, gracious and merciful provision is the rest of the story of forgiveness we seek to trace. Large parts of the books of Exodus, Leviticus, Numbers and Deuteronomy are concerned with how the broken relationship between God and his people can be managed and repaired. Today we focus on one aspect of this which was crucial for maintaining the life of God's people both corporately and individually: the arrangement for the 'sin-offering'.

The tabernacle, tent or temple were important places for Israel to encounter God. They were far richer meeting points than simply for sacrifice and forgiveness. They were places of worship and praise, for instruction and celebration, but nevertheless, as these texts indicate, dealing with breaches of God's laws was critical.

Verse 2 underlines one important feature of these instructions, namely that the sacrifices prescribed only relate to unintentional failures. They did not cover wilful sins. Often such deliberate breaches required the death penalty (e.g. Leviticus 20). It is equally important to note the arrangements for the Day of Atonement (Leviticus 16) which is 'an everlasting statute for you, to make atonement for the Israelites once in the year for all their sins' (16:34). 'For all their sins…' sounds completely comprehensive.

The directions for 'sin-offerings' cover various categories of people – 'anointed priests', 'the whole congregation', 'a ruler' and 'the ordinary people'. The prescribed 'sin-offering' suggests that the greater the privilege, the more demanding the sacrifice. At the heart of this process the offender lays his hand on the animal to be sacrificed, presumably identifying themselves with the sacrifice, and so indicating that the sacrifice is acting in their place. Even before this, it is often indicated that the person needs to acknowledge their guilt. There are also arrangements for those who cannot afford the costly animals initially prescribed (5:7–13). We can see here God's compassion and tender mercy, so that all can be included in the 'forgiveness'.

Finally, and perhaps most insightfully of all, is the repeated statement, 'The priest shall make atonement on your behalf for whichever of these sins you have committed, and you shall be forgiven' (5:13).

3 Forgiveness in the Psalms: the heart of the issue

Psalm 51 and 103:1–14

To many of us, it is a relief to move away from the legal rubrics and share in the heartfelt cry of Psalm 51. We might also find theological relief in the words of verses 16–17, 'For you have no delight in sacrifice… The sacrifice acceptable to God is a broken spirit.' With good reason this psalm has been the source of many a penitential prayer, although verses 18–19, with their confident statement that once Jerusalem is rebuilt God will delight in sacrifices, can be a challenge for us as well as Old Testament commentators!

This psalm also provides deep insight into the understanding of sin and the riches of forgiveness. Its association with David's brokenness when he is forced to face up to the reality of the evil he has committed against Uriah and his wife Bathsheba is understandable and appropriate, but the words, 'Against you, you alone have I sinned, and done what is evil in your sight' (v. 4), may strike anyone with awareness of the oppression of women as unacceptable. Surely he has wronged Bathsheba by seeing her naked, lusting after her and abusing his position as king to seduce her. He has also sought to corrupt Uriah and ultimately arranged for his assassination on the battlefield. It is definitely not the case that he has only sinned against God!

Then there is the claim, 'Indeed, I was born guilty, a sinner when my mother conceived me' (v. 5), which has led to another set of theological and pastoral issues, not to mention the moral dilemma as to whether he can then be held accountable, if his sinfulness is predetermined.

While both of these issues may be at least mitigated by claiming we are misunderstanding Hebrew idioms, they have certainly generated many controversies and been used oppressively.

More positively, we can note David's deep understanding of the outcome of sinning – that it casts us away from God's presence. This is the ultimate price of sin, as echoed in the garden of Eden account where Adam and Eve first hide from God and then are driven out of the garden. We shall see later that this is the cost to God as well, which he seeks to rectify at whatever price!

4 Forgiveness in the Psalms: the reality

Psalm 51:1–19; 32:1–11

We noted earlier that sacrifices were only prescribed for 'unintentional' or 'unwitting' sins. Psalm 103 proclaims, as a reason for blessing God, a larger reality: 'who forgives *all* your iniquity' (Psalm 103:3, my emphasis).

What sin is and what the equivalent form for forgiveness is, is well expressed in Psalm 32:1–2; however, it is Psalm 51 which presents the richest expressions. Below are the main ones I notice but there are even more expressions of the reality and experience of forgiveness for which the psalmist longs. The psalmist uses all these expressions not to differentiate types of sin but to underline the seriousness of sin which only God can deal with.

- *Blot out* my transgressions (v. 1)
- *Purge me* with hyssop, and I shall be clean (v. 7)
- *Wash me*, and I shall be whiter than snow (v. 7)
- *Hide your face* from my sins and *blot out* my iniquities (v. 9)
- Create in me a *clean heart* (v. 10)
- *Do not cast me away* from your presence (v. 11)
- *Deliver me* from bloodshed, O God, O God of my salvation (v. 14)

We focus on two of these. The first is 'blot out', which occurs twice (vv. 1, 9). We are familiar with the process of redacting documents to preserve identity, while allowing the crucial information to be seen. The corresponding term for 'sin' indicates rebellion against some authority with potentially life-threatening consequences (see 1 Kings 12:19 and 2 Kings 1:1). Here, therefore, it is not only the name but the whole case against the accused which is to be redacted. Some evidence for this background is provided by Nehemiah 13:14, where Nehemiah asks God not to blot out his good deeds.

The second is 'wash me'. Perhaps because of our baptismal rituals, this is a common picture we might use, but it is noteworthy that 'of all the penitential psalms… only Psalm 51 employs the language of washing' (W.P. Brown, *Seeing the Psalms*, John Knox Press 2002, p. 129). The image is not about a shower! It relates to washing clothes by treading on them repeatedly. This is before the days of detergents (although Jeremiah 2:22 indicates they had some aids) and washing machines. It recognises the difficulty of dealing with sin and implies the inadequacy of any superficial treatment.

5 Forgiveness in the prophets

Isaiah 1:1, 16–20; 6:1–13

The psalmist's plea was, 'Wash me, and I shall be whiter than snow'. Isaiah's God declares, '"Come now, let us settle the matter," says the Lord: "Though your sins are like scarlet, they shall be as white as snow; though they are red as crimson, they shall be like wool"' (1:18, NIV).

Here Isaiah pictures Israel in a courtroom situation – perhaps with their Suzerain accusing them of a breach of the covenant-treaty. Surprisingly, the Suzerain, rather than announcing punishment, offers them gracious and full forgiveness. The references to crimson and scarlet pick up on the hands full of blood which they stretch out before God (verses 15–16), but might also relate to the futile blood sacrifices they have offered (see verses 11–15). God's initial appeal was to 'wash yourselves' by turning from their evil behaviour and caring for the oppressed. Now God offers them another way if they respond. He will cleanse them.

It appears that Isaiah is agreeing with the psalmist, but there is an alternative understanding of these verses: 'If your sins are like scarlet, will they become like snow?' (1:18, NRSV). On this reading, God is saying their sacrifices are pointless and the only way to be restored is to fulfil the compassionate instructions of verses 15 and 16.

Isaiah does experience full, free and unexpected cleansing. In chapter 6, encountering the King, the Lord of Hosts (v. 5), the Holy God, Isaiah expects the worst. He has become acutely aware of his sin: a man of unclean lips, living among a people of unclean lips. He anticipates that the judgement book of God will condemn him.

The seraph touches his lips with a coal from the altar and announces, 'Your guilt has departed and your sin is blotted out' (v. 7). These could have been the words of the priest to someone making their sacrifice for unwitting sin, but now with total efficacy they are the words from the heavenly throne.

Why are lips the focus of his confession and the divine cleansing? Isaiah had earlier insisted that prayers were ineffectual and that actions are what count. Both Psalm 15 and 24 put right actions before right words, while recognising the importance of speech. Here the focus is on Isaiah's lips and speech, perhaps because of his call to speak for the Lord.

6 God's dilemma

Hosea 11:1–11; Isaiah 53:4–12; Jeremiah 31:31–34

Both Isaiah and Hosea before him realised there was a problem with sin. What if it became an addiction and, consequently, made it impossible for individuals or the nation to truly hear, repent and respond? Hosea's account of his relationship with Gomer, overlaid as it is with the rebellion of Israel, indicates that the point has been reached when Israel cannot any longer choose to return to God (see chapters 1—3). Isaiah's call includes the doom-laden message that, even though he speaks for God, the people cannot or will not respond appropriately to make restoration possible.

Yet there is a deeper message in the Bible too, that God's nature is such that he must find a way to enable forgiveness. Hosea's words convey God's dilemma: 'How can I give you up, Ephraim?… My heart recoils within me; my compassion grows warm and tender. I will not execute my fierce anger… for I am God and no mortal, the Holy One in your midst' (Hosea 11:8–9).

Yes, rebellion must be punished, but mercy is much greater. There is a similar message from God to Moses: 'The Lord, the Lord, a God merciful and gracious, slow to anger, and abounding in steadfast love and faithfulness, keeping steadfast love for the thousandth generation' (Exodus 34:6, 7), while punishment is only for four generations.

But how can God get round the problem of human wilful disobedience and rejection? Jeremiah describes one solution in the well-known new covenant, whereby God will reprogramme his people by putting his law within them: 'For I will forgive their iniquity, and remember their sin no more' (Jeremiah 31:31–34).

The later chapters of Isaiah offer an even deeper solution. Here, God's servant presents a puzzle. Yes, he is to be exalted and lifted up, but at the same time he is disfigured and rejected, despised. He is 'a man of suffering and acquainted with infirmity' (53:3). This servant was cut off from the land of the living, even though he had done no violence. And unlike Isaiah, there was no deceit in his mouth. What is going on? Has the moral order completely collapsed? Has evil ultimately conquered and crushed the good?

Somehow it is God's will to crush him with pain. Yet it is also the servant's choice because 'he poured out himself to death' through a process of identification with the transgressors (verses 11 and 12). Why? The end of verse 12 provides the answer!

Guidelines

- If someone asked you why bother reading Genesis 1—3, especially chapter 3, what could you share with them about the human need for forgiveness? Have you discovered anything new for yourself this week?

- Which aspects of forgiveness in the Old Testament have you found most surprising, most troublesome and most encouraging? Can you work out why you have responded as you have?

- Why do you think there is such an apparent disparity between the restriction of forgiveness in Leviticus to 'unwitting' or 'unintentional' sins and the sense of wholehearted and comprehensive forgiveness which we find in the Psalms? Is it entirely explicable by remembering that Leviticus was primarily from the priests' perspective and the Psalms allow us into the minds of people who have experienced forgiveness? Can we learn anything from this about our own mission of forgiveness?

- What are your favourite verses in the Psalms relating to forgiveness? Turn these into a prayer of confession and thanksgiving. Alternatively, reflect on a helpful prayer of confession or song about the experience of forgiveness. Use these to pray for yourself or help you understand why people you relate to may need to experience forgiveness.

1 The big picture

Mark 1:1–15

The Old Testament begins with good news, 'In the beginning when God created the heavens and the earth…' (Genesis 1:1) and goes on to explain how God brings order and beauty out of the swirling chaos. Mark begins his gospel by telling us, 'The beginning of the good news of Jesus Christ, the Son of God' (Mark 1:1). In Genesis it was God's word that brought order out of chaos. Now it is still God's word, but through his messenger John.

John appears not in Eden, but in the wilderness to which people have been driven. His task is to proclaim 'a baptism of repentance for the forgiveness of sins' (Mark 1:4). Yet this water baptism, powerful as it was, like John himself was the forerunner of something more powerful – baptism with the Holy Spirit (v. 8). Jesus is marked out as he receives the Spirit and by the voice designating him as God's Son, the beloved. Like Adam, Jesus goes through a period of testing – not in Eden but the wilderness. Like Adam and Eve, he is 'driven' there (Genesis 3:24). Now the scene is set. John is arrested, then Jesus appears proclaiming, 'The time is fulfilled…' It is time for the forgiveness of sins. God's new kingdom is now at hand.

It is probable that John expected the one who received the Spirit to usher in an age of judgement, as references to fire and trees cut down indicate (see Matthew 4:7–12; Luke 3:7–17). Certainly, John did not proclaim a message of unavoidable rejection, but people needed to repent if they were to be 'gathered into his granary' rather than being burnt with 'unquenchable fire', or avoid being chopped down (Matthew 3:10). Indeed, at the heart of his message was the reality of the forgiveness of sins as a preparation for belonging to the Messiah's kingdom. The mark of this forgiveness was baptism.

Jesus is depicted as being in continuity with John's message, in his demand to 'repent' (see Matthew 4:17; Mark 1:15), but maybe what is understood by this is rather different. Whereas John saw it as a radical demand to 'bear good fruit', what Jesus does is call people to follow him. Repentance for the four disciples does not appear to require sorrow for past sins, but a willingness to change the focus of their lives from violent revolution to the way of peace, from fishing and family to following Jesus (see Tom Wright, *Mark for Everyone*, SPCK, 2004, p. 9).

2 The controversy

Already in Mark's gospel Jesus has been demonstrating the nearness of God's kingdom by casting out demons and healing the sick. There are individuals in the Capernaum synagogue, Peter's mother-in-law and a 'leper'. There is also the general statement that he cured many and cast out many demons (1:34). Until now, not once has he mentioned repentance and forgiveness. So, this story is unusual in that the 'healing' involves the pronouncement that the paralysed man's sins are forgiven (v. 5). In this instance, Jesus doesn't require repentance as a precondition for forgiveness; rather, Jesus declares the man is forgiven. Matthew's version is more tender, 'Take heart, child: your sins are forgiven' (Matthew 9:2).

As the story unfolds, the evidence for this effective forgiveness is the man's healing! Precisely what Jesus' view is on the connection between sin and illness or forgiveness and healing is not made clear. In any case, some see this approach as essentially pastoral rather than theological; that the connection is in the paralytic's mind rather than necessarily being essentially true.

The key topic for this story, though, is not the man's miraculous healing. It is the controversy that Jesus' claim to forgive him initiates.

The objectors are named as scribes: the guardians of the law. The law taught that only God could forgive sins. Therefore, by implication Jesus was claiming to be God and so was guilty of blasphemy. Incidentally, the way forgiveness was 'obtained' was through the sacrificial system, which was controlled by the priests. Jesus was also, therefore, attacking this powerful group – as he did later in the temple (Mark 11:15–19, compare John 2:13–22). This clash contributed to his crucifixion.

But the central statement is in verse 10: 'So that you may know that the Son of Man has authority on earth to forgive sins…' Who these words were addressed to is not clear. They may have been for 'the scribes', or according to C.F.D. Moule, the gospel readers, i.e. the Christian community. In either case they establish that forgiveness is the gift of Jesus.

3 Human and divine

The Lord's Prayer is so familiar that we may easily forget how radical it is. 'And forgive us our debts' (verse 12a) seems such a simple prayer to the one who is our Father. Why, then, is this radical? From a Jewish perspective, potentially because no sacrifices seem to be involved! However, from a gospel perspective it is because Jesus makes our forgiveness dependent on us forgiving others: 'as we also have forgiven our debtors'. This was a core directive from Jesus to his disciples. He told a parable about the danger of not forgiving (Matthew 18:23–35). He amazed Peter by telling him he should forgive not just seven times but 'seventy-seven times', or even 'seventy times seven' (Matthew 18:21–22; compare Luke 17:4). This command to forgive others was taken up by Paul: 'Be kind to one another, tender-hearted, forgiving one another, as God in Christ has forgiven you' (Ephesians 4:32; compare Colossians 3:13).

In the Ephesians passage, our responsibility to forgive others is not so much a prerequisite for us to be forgiven, but rather a model and a motive. The word 'as' is more fully translated as 'just as' or 'even as'. We are probably correct if we limit the circle of forgiveness in these passages to the Christian community. But if we understand that Jesus died for the sins of the whole world and that his cry from the cross reaches out to all, then, if he is our model, there are ultimately no limits we can place on this requirement.

This emphasis both in the words of Jesus and within the New Testament on humans forgiving each other is in significant contrast to the Old Testament. I can find only two instances where this is noted or requested – namely Genesis 50:17 and 1 Samuel 25:28. It is of note that on both occasions it is an appeal to the wronged person not to retaliate or harm those who have offended them. It is not a divine command or a general condition for being forgiven.

Finally, we can consider where Jesus' 'condition' for our forgiveness might come from. Did it arise from the 'Year of Jubilee' when debts were released? Were these words an application of 'love your neighbour as yourself'? He insisted, 'Love your enemies and pray for those who persecute you' (Matthew 5:44). Even if this is not specifically telling us, 'Forgive those who persecute you,' it would seem to entail forgiveness.

4 The encounter

This is an account of terrible cruelty inflicted on a powerless person by those who ruled by immoral might. But in the midst of this brooding darkness, brought about by human protectionism, fear, cowardice, ruthless selfishness and also unquestioning obedience to those in authority, a light shines. We hear from the cross, from the dry lips of a tormented, rejected and vulnerable person, those unforgettable, almost unbelievable words from Jesus: 'Father, forgive them; for they do not know what they are doing' (Luke 23:34).

This shaft of light brings us hope in the darkest moment of human history, inspiring the words of John's gospel: 'The light shines in the darkness, and the darkness did not overcome it' (John 1:5). These are not words addressed to humans but to God. Even though the 'Son of Man has authority on earth to forgive sins' (Mark 2:10), Jesus is praying to his Father. This is a critical point in eternity. Here, above every other moment in Jesus' story, he both submits to and appeals to his Father to fulfil the purpose which brought him into our world. In Matthew's words, 'You are to name him Jesus, for he will save his people from their sins' (Matthew 1:21), or in Jesus' own words, 'The Son of Man came… to give his life a ransom for many' (Mark 10:45). It will for ever remain a mystery, but perhaps this moment is also the ultimate point of surrender to the Father's will: 'Not my will but yours be done' (Luke 22:42).

We must also consider the clause, 'for they do not know what they are doing'. Who is encompassed by 'they'? Luke has mentioned that 'the people stood by, watching; but the leaders scoffed at him' (Luke 23:35). In addition to these two groups we can add the soldiers who have crucified him, the disciples who have deserted him, denied him in Peter's case, and betrayed him in Judas'. Beyond these is Pilate and the mob who sealed his fate by crying, 'Crucify him'. Then the ripples go out to include us all, through all time and all space.

5 Forgiveness through Jesus (1)

Romans 3:19–26; Ephesians 1:3–10

Here are two dense passages that seek to illuminate our understanding of God's forgiveness. It may be a mystery (Ephesians 1:9) but it is something we can go at least some way to understanding. This mystery is 'set forth in Christ'. He is the key to God's action and our understanding.

According to Ephesians 1:7–8, 'We have redemption through his blood, the forgiveness of our trespasses, according to the riches of his grace that he lavished upon us.' And Romans 3:24–25 says: 'Now justified by his grace as a gift, through the redemption that is in Christ Jesus, whom God put forward as a sacrifice of atonement by his blood, effective through faith. He did this to show his righteousness, because in his divine forbearance he had passed over the sins previously committed.'

The Ephesians passage is significant in using the word for 'forgiveness', something the Pauline writings do not do very often. However, there are many links between these two passages, some of which we will note.

First, the medium for this process of redemption/forgiveness is 'through' or by his blood. Here we can recall the key verse in Leviticus 17:11: 'For the life of the flesh is in the blood; and I have given it to you for making atonement for your lives on the altar; for, as life, it is the blood that makes atonement.' Although the prompt for this verse is not a theory of atonement but rather why Israel is forbidden to eat any blood, it is nevertheless a key verse for our appreciation of Israel's understanding of the atonement process. When transferred to Jesus, while we might be tempted to understand 'the life of the flesh is in the blood' to mean it is his whole life which is the sacrificial process, the reference to 'on the altar' makes it clear that it his sacrificial death which is the focus.

Another link between these two passages is the emphasis on the gift nature of this process: 'the riches of his grace that he lavished upon us' and 'by his grace as a gift'. Both contain an emphasis on the unmerited nature of this gift of forgiveness and of its superabundance. No one could deduce from these passages that forgiveness is something we must wring out of God's hands. Like the father in Luke 15:20–24, he is looking and longing to offer forgiveness.

6 Forgiveness through Jesus (2)

1 John 1:5—2:6 [Our reflections focus on 2:1–2]

John provides us with a different perspective on the action of forgiveness. Here it is conditional on us acknowledging our sin. With Paul, this is also a necessary condition, as his rigorous arguments to establish 'all have sinned' indicate. But John underlines the importance of this recognition by pointing out that if we don't accept our sinfulness, we are making God a liar, which would be a very serious sin. As with Paul, John emphasises that in forgiving our sins God is being faithful and just. Paul's way of putting this is: 'He himself is righteous and that he justifies the one who has faith in Jesus' (Romans 3:26).

According to John, Jesus is 'the atoning sacrifice for our sins'. John emphasises later that the initiative is with God and that this 'atoning sacrifice' is the demonstration of his love (1 John 4:10). Some commentators highlight that 'the expression in 2:2 is wide enough to cover the whole work of Christ' (C.H. Dodd, *The Johannine Epistles*, Hodder & Stoughton 1946, p. 27), whereas others locate the 'atoning sacrifice' more precisely in the sacrificial death of Jesus.

As with Romans 3, so here there is considerable debate as to whether 'propitiate' or 'expiate' is the appropriate translation. In the end it becomes a debate about semantics – what exactly does 'propitiation' imply? Then the second issue is whether 'atoning sacrifice' is a proper and adequate translation for *hilasmos*. What is clear is that with John, as with Paul, forgiveness is not something we can procure from God by anything we might do, but rather the initiative and the effective remedy lies entirely with God himself.

Finally, we reflect on a further aspect of forgiveness, namely that Jesus is our 'advocate'. Perhaps we can sense that John is wanting us to understand two things. First, that the 'propitiation' is not an abstract or automatic process, generated by divine AI. It is real and personal. Secondly, that it is not only a historic event, in that it took place when Jesus was crucified, but also a living one, in which the risen Christ makes the impact of his death continuously effective. So, we need have no fears about its continuing efficacy for us.

Guidelines

Here are quotations from a classic dealing with our subject, Hugh R. Mackintosh, *The Christian Experience of Forgiveness* (Fontana, 1961), originally published in 1927. Please reflect personally on these and consider the implications for preaching, pastoral care and mission.

> *[Forgiveness] is experienced as that which passes all understanding... it is... the intervention of a love beyond all measure, a supernatural event not deducible by any human calculus... but rather the spontaneous and unanalysable deed of God... It emerges from pure love as an inexplicable gift to the unworthy which conveys the solution of our sorest problem... God has forgiven us and is our friend. (p. 38)*

> *He [Jesus] was not merely the supporter or spectator of pardon; he was... the mediator or agent. But he could not do his share in the conveyance of pardon to me except at a cost... And the cross born of this fraternal sympathetic agony in vicarious participation of human shame, is the climax... The bearer of forgiveness perishes in giving complete expression to the mercy and judgement which in their unity constitute the pardon of God. (p. 91)*

> *Repentance... like every religious act concerns the three cardinal modes of being conscious – knowing, feeling, willing. Sin is recognised, it is disliked, it is disowned. Recognition of sin... may be defiance... sorrow for sin... may be remorse or despair. Abandonment of sin by itself may be no more than prudence. The regenerating fact is all three, as a unity, baptised in a sense of God's personal grace to the sinful. (p. 202)*

FURTHER READING

In addition to the above which is available online, other studies are:

Vincent Taylor, *Forgiveness and Reconciliation* (MacMillan & Co., 1946).

Leon Morris, *The Cross in the New Testament* (Paternoster, 1976).

Derek Tidball, *The Message of the Cross* (IVP, 2001).

Russ Parker, *Forgiveness is Healing* (SPCK, 2011).

Use of the Old Testament in the New Testament

Rachel Tranter

There are numerous ways that references to the Old Testament are made and used in the New Testament, and different authors use very different methods. Moreover, there is ongoing, important debate over the relationship between how the New Testament authors used the Old Testament to clarify and defend the gospel and what the original Old Testament authors intended.

It is important to note that a New Testament writer's 'use' of the Old Testament is never simply limited to quotations, and assuming as such will severely weaken any study. As the terms used are many and varied, the ones I am using are defined as follows:

- Quotation: a series of words taken from the Old Testament.

- Allusion: something that references a person, a place or a literary work from the Old Testament.

- Echo: a type of allusion that invokes a notion or concept from the Old Testament.

These notes will investigate how the Old Testament is being used within the New Testament through two angles. First, we will look at this topic through three biblical books, each a different genre and written by different people: a gospel, one of Paul's letters and Revelation. The other angle is the type of use. Therefore we will look at quotations in Matthew, allusions in Ephesians and echoes in Revelation. This is, of course, not to say that these books only use the Old Testament in one way, but simply provides a helpful framework through which to look at the topic. Additionally, Matthew arguably uses quotations as his main way of engaging with the Old Testament; Paul mostly uses allusions, especially in Ephesians; and Revelation contains no quotations at all and most of its references are thematic instead of direct.

Bible quotations are taken from the NRSV.

1 'And you, Bethlehem'

Micah 5:2; Matthew 2:5–6

Here at the beginning of Matthew's gospel, in the birth narrative, we find the following used by Jerusalem's chief priests and scribes: 'And you, Bethlehem, in the land of Judah, are by no means least among the rulers of Judah; for from you shall come a ruler who is to shepherd my people Israel.' This is, at least to some extent, a quotation of Micah 5:2: 'But you, O Bethlehem of Ephrathah, who are one of the little clans of Judah, from you shall come forth for me one who is to rule in Israel, whose origin is from of old, from ancient days.'

Interestingly, despite the clear parallels, there are differences between these two quotes. First is the addition of the 'shepherd' phrase, which may well be drawn from 2 Samuel 5:2 ('It is you who shall be shepherd of my people Israel'). Matthew has conflated these two references, perhaps to emphasise the importance of the people of God. Indeed, in 2 Samuel, Israel is swearing allegiance to David following the death of Saul. Perhaps Matthew is suggesting that Jesus is the ultimate and rightful anointed king.

Second is the addition of 'by no means', which changes the meaning significantly. This blatant alteration is not necessarily a cause for concern, nor does it have to undermine Matthew's argument. Changing quotations from the Old Testament in this way is a technique also used by Qumran interpreters: the change is made to clarify what the interpreter sees as the true meaning. Matthew is viewing the text through the lens of subsequent revelation; Bethlehem was unimportant – *until* Christ came and changed its status. To reflect this, Matthew has also changed the quotation.

Furthermore, there are Jewish targums and other rabbinic literature which explicitly see Micah 5:2 as messianic prophecy. Matthew continues this tradition by deliberately weaving fulfilled Old Testament prophecies throughout his gospel, including this example, showcasing that so much of the Old Testament is pointing towards Jesus. Another example of this is the quotation of Zechariah 9:9 in Mathew 21:5: 'Tell the daughter of Zion, Look, your king is coming to you, humble and mounted on a donkey, and on a colt, the foal of a donkey.' This king, claims Matthew, is and always has been Jesus.

2 'My God, my God'

This quotation towards the end of Matthew is one of Jesus' well-known 'final sayings' from the cross. Though different gospels give us different final words, Matthew 27:46 goes as follows: 'And about three o'clock Jesus cried with a loud voice, *"Eli, Eli, lema sabachthani?"* that is, "My God, my God, why have you forsaken me?"' This is clearly a quotation from Psalm 22:1a: 'My God, my God, why have you forsaken me?'

Two things are noteworthy here. The first is that Matthew has used '*Eli, Eli*' for Jesus' words, while Mark uses '*Eloi Eloi*'. Mark's version is closest to the original Hebrew, whereas Matthew's is closest to the Aramaic vernacular of the time; Matthew was likely quoting how he would have heard Psalm 22 in his own language. This change does not need to lead us to doubt that the words themselves are genuine.

The second is that we don't know whether Jesus was uttering a cry of abandonment from the cross, or whether he was pointing to the whole psalm, which actually ends on a note of victory. Matthew does not explicitly tell us. There are various references to this psalm woven throughout this entire chapter – verse 35 (casting lots), verse 39 (passers-by shaking their heads) and finally this direct quotation – which might suggest that Matthew wants us to think of the whole psalm. However, while it may be similar to a Jewish midrash, where just the first line of something is quoted as a reference to the whole thing, abandonment is a key theme of Matthew, culminating in Jesus' (apparent) desertion by God. To disregard this narrative structure is disingenuous. We should be cautious in assuming that this is a cry of faith instead of abandonment.

Regardless, the use of this quotation from the Old Testament suggests that Matthew is typologically aligning Jesus and David, the author of the psalm, showing how even direct quotations can form part of an allusion. Once again, we are witnessing Matthew's conviction that the whole of Israel's history points forward to Jesus.

3 'All things under his feet'

Psalm 8:6; Psalm 110:1; Ephesians 1:20–22

By their very nature, allusions are harder to pin down. However, Ephesians 1:20 and 22 say the following: 'God put this power to work in Christ when he raised him from the dead and *seated him at his right hand* in the heavenly places… And he has put *all things under his feet* and has made him the head over all things for the church.' When compared to Psalm 110:1 and Psalm 8:6, we can see the clear allusions: 'The Lord says to my lord, '*Sit at my right hand* until I make your enemies your footstool'; 'You have given them dominion over the works of your hands; you have put *all things under their feet*' (all italics mine).

The phrase 'all things under his feet' could indeed simply allude to the 'footstool' in Psalm 110, instead of making use of a separate psalm. However, there are other instances where Paul has combined fragments from the psalms, so there is no reason to think that isn't the case here. On the other hand, it may be an allusion to Genesis 1, where the command to 'subdue' the earth is the same phrase, 'to put under your feet'. Perhaps we may argue that Paul had all three in mind. It is clear that Paul is deliberately using this provocative, messianic language to create in his readers' minds an association with the scriptural Messiah. The allusion to Psalm 110 is particularly interesting, as Jesus also interprets this psalm to be messianic (Mark 12:35–37), as likely would many Jewish interpreters at the time. Indeed, it is used frequently throughout the New Testament.

It is particularly interesting that Psalm 8's original meaning is to suggest that God has put all things under humanity's feet; that is, humanity as a whole has dominion. Paul restricts it here so that it is Christ, as the perfect human and the second Adam, who holds this power. So Paul is not just alluding to the Old Testament here, but he is also expanding and clarifying its meaning for his own time.

4 'Speak the truth' and 'do not sin'

Zechariah 8:16; Psalm 4:4; Ephesians 4:25–26

In Ephesians 4:25–26, we find: 'So then, putting away falsehood, let all of us *speak the truth* to our neighbours, for we are members of one another. Be angry but *do not sin*; do not let the sun go down on your anger.' We can see the allusions when we look at Zechariah 8:16 and Psalm 4:4: 'These are the things that you shall do: *Speak the truth* to one another, render in your gates judgements that are true and make for peace.' 'When you are disturbed, *do not sin*; ponder it on your beds, and be silent' (all italics mine).

Paul seems to be drawing from the wider context rather than just the verses themselves. For example, being faithful and truthful to each other was supremely important in exile (Zechariah 8:16), and that need for relational harmony is emphasised by Paul too (v. 25). While Zechariah 8 is concerned with the future conduct of Israel after their time of exile is over, Paul is concerned with the eschatological conduct of the new people of God. Similarly, for verse 26, it is likely that Paul was alluding to Psalm 4 more generally. In verse 25 he warns against lying, which the psalmist speaks against in Psalm 4:2, and Paul's command, 'Do not let the sun go down on your anger', is reminiscent of the psalmist's exhortation to 'ponder it on your beds', though clearly here Paul is not directly quoting the psalm.

Paul has not signposted or referenced the fact that either of these two phrases have come from the Old Testament. While some have argued that Paul's lack of signposting indicates that he is unconsciously using Old Testament language in his letters, the frequency with which he refers to the wider context of Old Testament quotations makes this unlikely. However, it is certainly true that Paul immersed himself in the language of the Old Testament and undoubtedly would have used it more frequently than his readers would have picked it up. Clearly Paul was drawing on these Old Testament ideas and images to clarify his arguments, in a similar way to Matthew's use of Old Testament prophecies.

5 The beast

Daniel 7; Revelation 13:1–8

Revelation stands apart from the rest of the New Testament in its use of the Old Testament as it contains no quotations whatsoever, despite having a greater number of references than any other New Testament book. As with allusions, echoes are even more far removed from the original text, taking ideas and images from scripture instead of linking directly to any one verse or book. Some examples include echoes of the plagues of Egypt in John's trumpet and bowl judgements (Revelation 16); echoes of Genesis 1—3 (creation/fall) throughout Revelation; and the echo of the fall of Babylon (Ezekiel 26—28) in Revelation 18.

The book of Daniel is important in the book of Revelation; in proportion to its length, there are more references to Daniel than any other Old Testament book. Of these, most come from Daniel 7, the most noteworthy of which are in the description of the beast in Revelation 13.

Revelation 13:1–8 contains clear allusions to the beast in Daniel 7 (coming from the sea, having ten horns/heads, being compared to various animals). But we find many echoes here too. The four animals in Daniel 7 become just one beast in Revelation 13. There are also thematic links, such as the fact that the beast is given authority (v. 4; compare Daniel 7:6, 'dominion was given to it'), that beast gets this authority for 42 months (v. 5; compare Daniel 7:25, 'a time, two times, and half a time') and that the beast speaks blasphemies against God (v. 6; compare Daniel 7:25, 'He shall speak words against the Most High... shall attempt to change the sacred seasons and the law'). Verse 5 could be said to be a collective allusion as it draws on many different verses in Daniel 7.

Because of the density of Old Testament echoes here, and indeed the number of different places John might be drawing from, it's possible that his language may be unconscious as a result of his familiarity with Old Testament language. As with this argument for Paul, I disagree that this is the case. There are links between the Old Testament contexts of the chapters referenced; these 'clusters' seem deliberate. While there are some that may be unconscious, it is clear that John deliberately drew on Old Testament language, and, especially here in Revelation 13, Daniel 7 was a primary influence.

6 'New heavens and new earth'

Isaiah 65:17–19; Revelation 21:1–4

Another echo that John makes good use of in Revelation is the image of the New Jerusalem. Compare Revelation 21 with Isaiah 65: 'Then I saw a new heaven and a new earth; for the first heaven and the first earth had passed away' (Revelation 21:1). 'For I am about to create new heavens and a new earth; the former things shall not be remembered or come to mind' (Isaiah 65:17). Read these passages in full if you can.

We can see that the concept of 'new heavens and a new earth' has been taken by John and expanded. Some of the ideas are similar to this Isaiah passage, but others appear to be drawn from different sources. For example, the imagery of the bride is used frequently throughout Isaiah to represent the kingdom of Israel, including in 61:10 ('as a bride adorns herself with her jewels') and 62:5 ('as the bridegroom rejoices over the bride, so shall your God rejoice over you'). We also see this reference 'cluster' again, as John has drawn language from elsewhere in Isaiah, Daniel 7 and Ezekiel 40—48.

It might be helpful to see Revelation as a work of intertextuality: the meaning of the Old Testament text is changed by being put into a new context. In this way, John is taking aspects of the Old Testament scriptures, but he is not directing our attention towards the original context in the way that Matthew does through quotations or Paul does through his use of allusions. John isn't necessarily interpreting the Old Testament, but instead is using its language and images to make his own theological point or to clarify his prophetic vision. Thus, there is a relationship between John's words and the words of the Old Testament, but it is not as simple as engaging with the Old Testament context afresh. The meaning of the Old Testament is expanded and taken in a new direction in Revelation, and it achieves this through allusions and echoes that are used very differently to the rest of the New Testament.

Guidelines

We have seen a variety of quotations, allusions and echoes that have been used throughout the Old Testament. Many of the uses of the Old Testament I have examined here work to expand, change or develop their meaning. The New Testament writers viewed the Old Testament scriptures through the lens of Christ's life, death and resurrection. We must remember that the New Testament writers were not attempting to use the Old Testament in a regulated way; they were simply using everything at their disposal to prove and demonstrate the new 'Way' that had come to light through Christ and to encourage the fledgling church in its faith.

Ultimately, some uses of the Old Testament in the New Testament will have to remain a mystery – as indeed the New Testament writers described the gospel itself. However, we can look at Old Testament context, New Testament context and Jewish exegesis to gain some understanding of what the New Testament writers are doing. They add layers of meaning to texts, drawing our attention to different aspects of Old Testament prophecy and writings, and by paying careful attention to this we can more fully understand and appreciate their writings.

FURTHER READING

G.K. Beale and D.A. Carson (eds), *Commentary on the New Testament Use of the Old Testament* (Baker Academic, 2007).

John Goldingay, *Reading Jesus's Bible: How the New Testament helps us understand the Old Testament* (Eerdmans, 2017).

Stanley N. Gundry (ed.), *Three Views on the New Testament Use of the Old Testament* (Zondervan, 2008).

Steve Moyise, *The Old Testament in the New: An introduction* (T&T Clark, 2015).

Stanley E. Porter, *Sacred Tradition in the New Testament: Tracing Old Testament themes in the gospels and epistles* (Baker Academic, 2016).

The poetry of the Magnificat

Elizabeth Dodd

Mary's song of praise has been part of the fabric of Christian faith and worship since before the four gospels were written down. Recited every day in western and eastern traditions of daily prayer, it takes on particular significance in the season of Advent and the Feast of the Visitation on 31 May. It has provided inspiration for countless Christian prayers, hymns and poems from Thomas Tallis to 'Tell out, my soul'.

The Magnificat is significant as one of the few examples of original poetry in the New Testament. Like any good poem, this text cannot be reduced to a single meaning. It is written in Greek but in a Hebrew style, echoing the hymns, psalms and prophecies of the Hebrew Bible. It draws on stories of childless women given their heart's desire and of victories won through God's strength. It's significant that it is sung by a woman, giving rare insight into the heart of a female character as well as a powerful declaration of salvation for all Israel. It is also a window into the heart of scripture, into the chants and songs that provided the building blocks for the later written text.

Familiarity breeds contempt, and it has often been said that the revolutionary power of this poem has been lost through endless repetition. We can recover some of its impact by peeling back its layers of meaning. This week will reflect on the Magnificat in the context of Luke's infancy narrative and against the background of the Hebrew scriptures that inspired it. It will be read as a song of victory, a prophetic poem and a hymn of praise, one designed to be recited and repeated throughout the generations.

Unless otherwise stated, Bible quotations are taken from the NRSV.

1 A window into Mary's heart

Luke 1:26–56

In biblical histories and stories, lyric poems like Mary's song often work like an interlude that intersperses the narrative. In the middle of what might be a bare and factual story, lyrics create a moment of emotional intensity and provide a window into the characters' thoughts and feelings. Mary's song is a lyric in this classic sense. The opening lines in Luke 1:46–47 declare this expression of joy to be the outpouring of Mary's very 'soul' and 'spirit', an intimate picture of her state of mind.

When we read it in the context of the story of Luke 1, it is striking that this hymn comes a little while after Mary receives the news of her pregnancy. There is a process between acceptance of the task set before her and finding joy in it. The Greek term for 'went with haste' in verse 39 could carry a sense of threat and fear. Mary does not hurry to her elder cousin Elizabeth to share in the joyful expectation of children, but to seek support in an anxious and difficult time. Mary's hymn comes only after Elizabeth's prophetic exclamation in verses 41–45, in which she confirms that Mary's situation is of God. As a response to this encouragement Mary's song appears as a release of emotion, a confession of hope that can now be spoken in the presence of one who loves and supports her.

The hope that is expressed here is a remarkable one in the light of the precariousness of Mary's situation. The declaration of verse 48, 'Surely from now on all generations will call me blessed', might be seen as highly optimistic given the dangers that faced a pregnant woman at this time, particularly one who was young and unmarried. Why does this hymn appear at this point in the story, early on in Mary's pregnancy, and not after Jesus' birth? The answer to this question says much about the character of Mary as well as the nature of the hope of salvation.

2 A woman's triumph

Luke 1:5–25, 39–45; 1 Samuel 2:1–10

Alongside Mary, the other important character in Luke 1 is Elizabeth. Although most of the story concerns her husband Zechariah, it is Elizabeth who (like Mary) responds to the miracle of grace with faith and prophetic insight. Regarding her own unexpected pregnancy, she rejoices that the Lord has 'looked favourably on me and took away the disgrace I have endured among my people' (v. 25). In some early versions of Luke's gospel it is Elizabeth, not Mary, who then goes on to speak the longer song of praise in verses 46–55 (see notes to v. 46).

The parallels between Luke 1:46–55 and 1 Samuel 2:1–10 come out much more strongly when the Magnificat is heard as the praise song of an older woman who has seen the unexpected fulfilment of lost hope in giving birth to a child. Unlike the confident optimism of the younger voice, the elder carries the weight and pain of history. It reverberates with the rapture of a long struggle of faith finally vindicated. This is a joy made more painfully intense by the understanding that comes from experience, that much of the time such miracles do not occur.

On this reading, the exaltation of the 'lowly' that is a major theme in both texts is a reminder of the shame unjustly imposed on childless women, then and now (Luke 1:48, 51–3; 1 Samuel 2:4–5, 8). The fierceness of Hannah's exultation sounds at times more like a song of victory than a prayer of thanksgiving. Compared to the more delicately poetic 'He has scattered the proud in the imagination of their hearts' (Luke 1:51), Hannah appears to enjoy an almost vindictive triumph over the 'enemies' who have derided her (1 Samuel 2:1b).

The dramatic imagery of military, social and economic reversals that appears in both texts is perhaps more than poetic licence (Luke 1:51–53; 1 Samuel 2:4–5). Like the Magnificat, Hannah's song predates the story to which it has become attached. It may be one of the oldest psalms (indeed one of the oldest texts) in the Hebrew Bible. Some scholars have highlighted the incongruousness of applying a military song to a story about infertility. However, placed in these stories, the metaphorical world of these poems connects the struggles of forgotten women with the struggles of a nation, their personal triumphs with those of their community. Their God is the God of all who are downtrodden or neglected.

3 A song of victory

Today's reading is an ancient Hebrew poem. Victory songs like this were traditionally sung by women welcoming men home from battle, but the song of Deborah subverts expectations as Deborah is not just the singer but also a victor in the tale. Deborah is the only named female judge of Israel, a woman of power and authority, a prophet and military leader who brought peace through victory in battle. The previous chapter tells the story of this poem, how Deborah summons Barak to battle against the Canaanites. He agrees to go only if she accompanies him, and she prophesies that victory over the general Sisera will not be his, but 'the Lord will sell Sisera into the hand of a woman' (Judges 4:9). Chapter 5's ballad of victory, won by the hand of a woman, can be read as a celebration of female agency or as an assertion that God wins the victory despite the cowardice and faithlessness of men.

One of the high points of Deborah's song is a graphic description of the death of the enemy general Sisera at the hands of the woman Jael (vv. 24–27). The repetition in verse 27 acts almost like a chorus that emphasises the enormity of the event. This episode raises difficult questions about violence and female sexuality. Both the poem and the narrative version (Judges 4:17–22) seem to revel in the violence of the affair. This is one of a number of stories in the Hebrew Bible in which women use violence, sexuality or deceit for the cause of Israel and the honour of God (e.g. Esther 5:1–3; Judith 13:1–6). How does it affect our reading of the Magnificat to imagine stories such as this as its background and inspiration?

Verse 7 proclaims Deborah as a 'mother in Israel'. As feminist commentator J. Cheryl Exum has pointed out Deborah does not display motherly traits of nurturing, kindness or forbearance. She is a protector and a liberator, one who safeguards her people's future. It is instructive to reflect on the Mary of the Magnificat in similar terms, as a mother of Israel, drawing on a long heritage of women who have revealed the power of God to save God's people.

4 A prophetic cry

Luke 1 casts Elizabeth and Mary as prophetic figures, and Mary's song can be read as a prophetic poem (1:41, 45). Today we are reading one of the most ancient prophetic poems of the Hebrew Bible. Although the longer version of Exodus 15:1–18 has been attributed to Moses, it is possible that these words belong to the prophet Miriam, and not only the truncated version of verse 21.

The poetic power of scriptural prophecy has long been recognised, from Robert Lowth's lectures on Hebrew poetry (1754) to the popular work of Walter Brueggemann today. Prophecy's poetic form is significant for several reasons. Firstly, poetry's heightened language can evoke an ecstatic or trance-like feeling which suggests that these are words inspired by the Spirit of God. The exuberant display of tambourines and dancing in Exodus 15:20 also contributes to this ritualised expression of empowerment by the Spirit. Secondly, there is a rhetorical, persuasive aspect to poetry that is crucial to the prophet's task, as they set out not just to inform people about the will of God but to inspire them to action.

Prophecy does not just predict the future but seeks to unfold the heart of God for the present. From this perspective, one of the most interesting features of Hebrew poetry is its mixing of tenses. English translations may smooth over the differences, but Hebrew often jumps between past and present, perfect and imperfect verbs. So, although the NRSV renders Luke 1:46–47 all in the present tense, it is better translated (all italics mine): 'My soul *magnifies* the Lord, and my spirit *has rejoiced* in God my Saviour.' Similarly, there is an ambiguity in Exodus 15:13: should this read 'In your steadfast love you *led* the people whom you redeemed' (NRSV) or '… you *will lead* the people you have redeemed' (NIV)? The narrative difficulty here is that verses 13–18 refer to events that have not yet happened in the story. The people of Israel have just emerged from the Red Sea; they have not yet crossed the Jordan or defeated the surrounding nations.

As we see in Luke 1:46–55, there is power in declaring future events in the 'prophetic perfect tense', as if they are already accomplished. This goes beyond expressing hope and trust in the fulfilment of the purposes of God. It seems for a moment to step outside history, presenting a vision before our eyes of a time when all injustice will end and God's kingdom will reign.

5 A hymn to be sung

Luke 1:67-79; 2:13-14, 28-32

It has often been said that Hebrew has no word for 'poetry', and that the Hebrew texts we read as poems are better understood as songs that have lost their music. The Magnificat is one of four songs in the opening chapters of Luke that were probably sung or chanted by the early church. The songs of Zechariah, the angels and Simeon in Luke 1—2 may, like the Magnificat, have already been in circulation before the gospel of Luke was recorded.

The liturgical background of these poems is a reminder of the traditions of worship that lie behind much of the biblical text and its witness. Through poems like these we get a glimpse into the soul of early Christian devotion. These heartfelt cries of praise are the voice of an oral culture and of a living tradition that have the potential to subvert the at-times patriarchal overtones of Luke as an authoritative narrator. The fact that Zechariah's song validates Mary's prophecy, or that Simeon speaks while Anna speaks not at all, does not negate the powerful impact of hearing a song of praise from the mouth of a woman.

In western traditions of daily prayer these songs are heard separately: the Benedictus in morning prayer, the Magnificat and song of Simeon in evening prayer or compline. Set alongside each other, we hear the similarities and differences of message, form and voice all the more clearly. Simeon's well-known phrase 'now you are dismissing your servant in peace' (2:29) is perhaps better translated, 'now you are liberating your slave'. Mary, Zechariah and Simeon share a theme of liberation, which seems to reveal more in common between the hopes of these old men and young woman than is immediately apparent.

Interpreted as psalms, these songs not only add colour to the narrative but provide a guide for devotion to the Christ-child who is being revealed. They are not tied to the stories in which we find them. Instead we are positively invited to speak the 'I' for ourselves, to imagine the 'we' as that of our own community. What do these words mean for us today, and who is the Christ that they reveal, for our time?

6 A new song

Having spread our gaze across the story that surrounds it, the songs that inspired it and the communities that have sung it, we now turn back to the Magnificat as a poem. Poetry is many things but above all, perhaps, it is beautiful. This beauty has a power that can be seen in the great art, poetry and music that the Magnificat has inspired: from Botticelli to Rainer Maria Rilke to Arvo Pärt.

We have seen how this poem draws from a rich well of history and tradition, but it is also a new song (see Psalm 40:3). For Walter Brueggemann, the poems of Luke 1—2 are the best and only way to announce the new order of the kingdom of heaven (*Prophetic Imagination*, pp. 50–51). In these songs, the rational logic of empire is resisted and overthrown through the musical logic of poetry. The revolutionary force of this vision is felt through the tools of the poet's art, the craft of language.

This poem is structured into two major strophes (46b–50, 51–55). Closer study also reveals patterns of rhythm and rhyme that impel the reader forward and bind the words together. The first half centres on Mary's personal response to God, the second on the fate of Israel. Together these two halves unite the heart of a woman and the heart of a nation, beating together in joy and hope.

Hebrew poetry is most popularly associated with semantic parallelism, a rhyming of sense rather than sound. Verses 46–47 demonstrate synonymous parallelism, where the second line repeats the meaning of the first line in different words. Here, repetition invites the reader to dwell in the depths of Mary's astonished joy. Verses 52–53 demonstrate antithetical parallelism, where one line is followed by another with an opposite sense. This device measures the gulf between the ways of God and the ways of the world. There is also a chiastic or symmetrical structure to these lines (a-b-b-a) that draws attention to the miraculous and unexpected nature of God's transformation of society.

As the poem builds to its climax, the tone shifts from the contemplative/thankful first strophe to the purposeful/determined second. Verses 51, 52 and 54 all begin with strong active verbs ('he has shown', 'he has brought', 'he has come'). Whatever our view of Mary, her song ends in strength. Hers is a new song that celebrates God's power erupting into the world.

Guidelines

In 2012 the British artist Jenny Saville adapted Leonardo da Vinci's famous cartoon of Mary and the infant Jesus in a sketch called *Reproduction drawing IV*, which shows two identical mother-figures trying to contain a wriggling child who will not sit still. The artist has captured the movement by drawing and redrawing the infant, who seems to be split into at least three separate bodies, hands and legs everywhere like a blurred photograph.

The Magnificat is a bit like this. It has been many things to many people. Mary's voice has been heard as one of meek acceptance, youthful hope, prophetic vision or a revolutionary call to arms. Like the child in Saville's drawing, the hope that Mary carries is both tangible and elusive, known and unknown, deeply felt while belonging to an imagined future.

One of the great advantages of poetic language is its capacity for ambiguity. A poetic word can easily mean ten things at once without contradiction. This week presents an opportunity to review your relationship with this poem, what it has meant to you in the past and what it might mean for you today.

- Imagine yourself into the nativity story. How does the Magnificat speak to you in the light of Mary's situation at the time?

- Read it first in the voice of Mary and then of Elizabeth. How do the words resonate differently?

- Try reading it as: a victory song, a prophecy and a hymn of praise. What jumps out at you in each reading?

- Explore some different poetic, musical or artistic interpretations of the Magnificat. What new insights have you found in the text?

- Recall one of the most joyful or exultant times in your life. Craft a prayer that expresses your feelings to God.

FURTHER READING

Robert Alter, *The Art of Biblical Poetry* (Basic Books, 2011).

Walter Brueggemann, *The Prophetic Imagination* (Fortress Press, 2018).

F.W. Dobbs-Allsopp, *On Biblical Poetry* (Oxford University Press, 2015).

J. Cheryl Exum, 'Mother in Israel' in Letty M. Russell (ed.), *Feminist Interpretation of the Bible* (The Westminster Press, 1985), pp. 73–85.

Barbara Reid, Shelly Matthews and Amy-Jill Levine, *Luke 1—9* (Liturgical Press, 2021).

Finding Jesus in the world

Cally Hammond

After we become Christians, we see the world differently. But when faith goes against popular attitudes, not everyone shares our vision. At this time of year, the world around us is giving us one message, while our faith tells us something different. In the world, everything is getting darker. The working day begins and ends in gloom. We stay indoors to escape from the chill and dark. Plants die down, gardens settle into dormancy. The air is colder, the weather more miserable. Leafy trees turn to skeleton silhouettes.

Christian life and Christian worship follow an alternative path. If we use lectionary readings for the year, they are now pointing us towards thinking about new beginnings, just at the season when the calendar year draws to a close. In particular, we are encouraged to see signs of the coming kingdom of God. But how can this make sense to us amidst the darkness and chill of looming winter?

This is a good time to remember that Christianity is a topsy-turvy, back-to-front, upside-down faith. Paul is the first Bible writer to focus on this: 'whenever I am weak, then I am strong' (2 Corinthians 12:10), he writes. Death becomes life eternal for those who belong to Jesus, for the mortal body of a believer will become immortal (Romans 8:11).

Of all the topsy-turvy ideas in our faith, the starkest is surely the new meanings of 'life' and 'death'. They normally seem to be utterly, inevitably opposed to each other. Yet in the Christian proclamation, death means life, and life means death. Jesus puts it like this: 'unless a grain of wheat falls into the earth and dies, it remains just a single grain, but if it dies it bears much fruit' (John 12:24). He was talking about himself. But he was thinking of us too.

Unless stated otherwise, Bible quotations are taken from the NRSV.

1 In the end, a beginning

Revelation 21:1–27

We like what we know. That's not surprising: familiarity helps us to feel safe, in our homes, and in our communities and country, where language, people, customs, food and all the little markers of identity are familiar.

The Bible, however, teaches that we are travellers in this world. Our future lies elsewhere. It gives us some clues about this unknown future so not everything will be unfamiliar. We know we shall meet our loved ones again (1 Thessalonians 4:17; John 14:4). Here in Revelation, there is a picture of the holy city, a new Jerusalem, to encourage us. It dazzles with crystal, pearls, gold and precious stones (vv. 11–21).

It can feel awkward, then, admitting that even the beauty of heaven may not be enough to make us look forward to going there. What we know of it is based on the few ideas the Bible gives us and on the vision of others. For the present, it is foreign to us. We are not ready to be called there, for we still have work to do in this world.

One clue about heaven comes when John tells us that 'the sea was no more' (v. 1). He was living in exile, so the sea divided him from his home and loved ones. Heaven will end such divisions. He endured suffering, but in his vision, the Lord promises him that grief, pain and death will be no more. We often turn to verses 3–4 for comfort and hope when we are bereaved or suffering.

Christ makes all things new. But even in heaven he bears the marks of the nails from his crucifixion. They reassure us that in heaven we will still be us. Sanctified and justified, yes, but still us. At the end of the year it's good to pray to be ready to meet Christ when he comes. This doesn't mean living each day in perpetual anxiety. God is not expecting perfection. All he asks is that we love one another (John 13:34–35), for then we have taken to heart the blessed assurance of life eternal.

2 In darkness, light

Every farmer, every gardener, knows that without light there is no growth. Every Christian knows that in scripture light stands for good and dark for evil. That is the message of the Psalms (18:28; 27:1; 119:105).

Light has two elements to it, each playing its part in waking the dormant seed, the dormant soul. First, light means warmth. If we change a lightbulb when it is switched on, we will burn our fingers. To human beings, warmth is life, for we call ourselves 'warm-blooded'.

Second, light illuminates. We use technology to break down the light/dark barrier. Thus our working day can extend beyond the boundaries of dawn and dusk. Shift workers sleep in the daytime. Hospitals and other essential services work 'round the clock'. Despite this, our use of language has not changed. Christians use the language of illumination for God, while darkness suggests God's absence.

Light matters to Jesus, so it follows that it matters to John too. He writes that 'the light shines in the darkness, and the darkness has not overcome it' (v. 5, RSV). In his first letter, he adds, 'God is light and in him there is no darkness at all' (1 John 1:5). Darkness brings fear in its wake because we are deprived of one of our physical senses. Then two things can help us. One is to wait until our eyes adjust and make the most of what little light there is. The other is to increase our reliance on our senses of hearing and touch.

Understood like this, darkness at the year's ending is not a danger but an opportunity. We have a chance to refresh our vision by relying on those other perceptions instead. Most of us are terrible at listening. So this can be a time to practise listening – to God, and to other people. Perhaps a bit more attention will help us see what they really mean or need.

Matthew's gospel says that we are 'the light of the world' (Matthew 5:14). This makes us Christ-like; for Jesus too is 'the light of the world' (John 8:12).

3 In people, God

Christians are not free from self-centredness. We can be just as self-obsessed as any non-Christian. Faith calls us to grow in grace, to be constant in prayer, to study the scriptures. Yet even as we strive to fulfil these ideals, we can miss the mark. Even the Bible can become a temptation, if striving for biblical knowledge tips over into arrogance as we think we have privileged access to God. Then if we look in a mirror, it is not ourselves that we see reflected; it is Luke's Pharisee in the temple (Luke 18:11) who stares back at us.

Rabbi Lionel Blue once said that hypocrites look after their own bodies and other people's souls; whereas genuinely religious people look after their own souls and other people's bodies. This made me smile. I realised how well his words reflect the parable of the sheep and the goats. If we met someone who was lonely, hungry or thirsty, we might decide to help them. But if we met someone who was lonely, hungry or thirsty – and famous, most of us would be a bit more eager to help. And if we discovered that God incarnate was in the lonely, hungry, thirsty person, we would fall over ourselves to help them.

But the point of Jesus' story in Matthew 25 is that God is in all the lonely, hungry, thirsty people we ever meet; and that every time we help another person, we honour and love the Lord. This is daunting. Who has enough time, money, willingness to be taken for a fool, to show such universal love?

Christ does. I used to worry about how to decide how to respond when I became aware of someone in need. But I listened to St Augustine, who says that we cannot do all the good everyone needs all the time, so we should focus our attention on those God puts in our path. Make choices, love to the best of our abilities and leave the outcome with God, who knows the thoughts of our hearts, including our feelings of inadequacy.

4 In judgement, mercy

James targets a problem which Christians have struggled with right from the beginning. How can we live in a proper relationship with God? Most of us would cherish Paul's message that we are made righteous by our faith in God, and not by 'works' (Galatians 2:16).

We all meet people who rely on their works to save them, living lives of conspicuous morality, ostentatiously avoiding sin and temptation. And we all know people who, without reading their Bible, saying their prayers or going to church, have a transformative effect on others by the self-giving – and frankly Christ-like – goodness of their lives.

Having faith, and grace, and the Spirit, ought to change us. The old hymn says, 'the vilest offender who truly believes, that moment from Jesus a pardon receives' (Fanny Crosby, 1820–1915). But from that moment on, our lives must be different to be truly Christian. If they are not filled with Spirit-led goodness, then even though Christ has redeemed us, we are still shutting him out of our hearts, our lives, our world.

James cuts through complex theological language of grace, predestination, salvation and redemption. He was a straightforward kind of person, for whom following Jesus was equally straightforward. 'Don't listen to what people say,' he warns. 'Look at how they behave.' He tells us that we are to be judged by the 'law of liberty,' but that is not a free pass to do what we like. It is an invitation to grow up into 'the measure of the full stature of Christ' (Ephesians 4:13).

If we are honest, we must confess that sometimes we fall short of that 'full stature'. Of course we do, for we are not Christ. We are 'only human'. But we can treat this season of gathering darkness as an opportunity to turn our behaviour around and strive to be the person Christ calls us to be. Not by ticking boxes on a moral checklist, but by learning to love others, as he first loved us.

5 In weakness, majesty

Zechariah 9:1–17

Everyone experiences the coming of winter as increasing darkness. But there is another kind of darkness. It can form within us. Some people are so badly affected by the lack of light that it triggers an emotional darkness in them, dulling their senses, flattening emotions, damping down expectation.

There is a medical element to this melancholy ('seasonal affective disorder' or SAD). It may be labelled as a form of 'depression,' a word which evokes the heavy weight pressing them down. Such sadness can be distressing. People feel unable to help themselves, and are not helped by others saying, 'try harder' or 'cheer up'.

In Zechariah, we find a better way of dealing with pressure and distress. The Lord turned away from his people because they were disloyal and disobedient. They endured suffering and desolation, but their suffering will not last forever. Their Lord is coming to the rescue.

Through the prophet, God gives his people a gift, a message of hope, wrapped in powerful words. When they unwrap it, they find a surprise. It is not weapons to defeat their enemies, nor a powerful leader to stir their courage and urge them on to victory. The gift God gives them is a king.

This king does not ride a war horse. He rides a donkey, a humble beast of burden. He will do away with all weapons, but he will not leave his people unprotected. Instead he says, 'No more!' to violence of every kind and to war: and his message speaks both to his ancient people and to all the nations. For he is the one true God of all.

Some solutions are useless, even positively unhelpful, like telling a person who is depressed to cheer up. Then God steps in and takes us in hand. Instead of giving us fire-power to equal our enemies, he changes our situation so completely that the old solutions vanish along with the old problems. We need not fear the melancholy darkness or its crushing weight. Our king is coming to save us, to be born as one of us. He will make all things new, even the world itself.

6 At the close, an opening

Revelation 3:8–22

Soon, another year of Christianity will become history, as the page of the book of life turns. A fresh page waits to be filled with the stories of Christians yet to come. If we look back at the year now passing, we will see times when we have failed in faith. We realise that we need to work on faults which are turning into habits.

The Lord warns us to expect a reproof for this (v. 19). That will hurt, for we really do love him and want to serve him. He reveals himself as the 'light of the world' (John 8:12), standing at the door and knocking. Amid the darkness, he brings light into our homes and hearts. So light is not merely a matter of science, of physics. To us, the light is a person, Jesus Christ.

Christ is knocking, as if he longs to come in and abide with us. But we are standing behind the closed door, scarcely breathing, wondering what to do next. If we stay still and do nothing, he may go away, and we will be left in darkness forever. If we open the door, nothing in our lives will stay the same – and we fear what we do not know.

This is one of those times when one part of the Bible speaks directly to another. Revelation 3 makes deeper sense to us when we read it in the light of Matthew 7:7–8. There Jesus says:

'Ask, and it will be given you; search, and you will find; knock, and the door will be opened for you. For everyone who asks receives, and everyone who searches finds, and for everyone who knocks, the door will be opened.'

Jesus is talking about us, as we journey through our world in search of God. This time he is not knocking at our door asking us to let him in. Instead, we are knocking at his door. And that gospel verse promises us that when we do, the door will always be opened, and then, at last, we shall come home.

Guidelines

Just as we outgrow our clothes in childhood, and have to hand them down to others or throw them away, so our first garment of faith has to be changed as we are weaned off spiritual milk and get stuck into the solid food of faith. Tastes also change. What suited us when we were young may come to seem too sweet, too spicy or too bland. We cannot wear the same garment of faith all our lives, or eat the same diet of spiritual milk.

The world is not our enemy, but it is full of challenges for the grown-up Christian. As we encounter new ideas and things, our faith has to make room for them.

We mark the turning of the year as individuals (birthdays), all together as a people (1 January) and as the church (Advent Sunday). Each is an opportunity to take stock. Have we outgrown our old ways of being Christians? Do we need to find a new place to worship, a new habit of Bible reading? Do we need to refresh our prayer life by exploring meditation, or simply silence?

One useful tip I learned from a nun over 30 years ago was not to try to swallow a passage of scripture whole. Read a passage, and reflect, and wait to see what verse or message comes to the surface. Then take that as your message for the day, and turn it over in your mind repeatedly, letting it speak to you. You can also do this by taking the hardest, most obscure or difficult verse, if you are feeling up for a challenge.

If I had to choose one verse from each of the six readings we have shared this week, it would be these: Revelation 21:6; John 1:5; Matthew 25:34; James 2:13; Zechariah 9:10; Revelation 3:10. Now you choose yours!

FURTHER READING

David Adam, *Love the World* (SPCK, 2018).

Cally Hammond, *Joyful Christianity: Finding Jesus in the world* (SPCK, 2009).

Margaret Silf, *Lighted Windows: An Advent calendar for a world in waiting* (BRF, 2016).

David Kerrigan, *The Prince of Peace in a World of Wars: Applying the message of God's love to a needy world* (BRF, 2018).

John Sweet, *Revelation (New Testament Commentaries)* (SCM Press, 1979). This book is out of print but available second-hand via **abebooks.co.uk**.

Tom Wright, *Advent for Everyone: A journey with the apostles* (SPCK, 2017).

SHARING OUR VISION – MAKING A GIFT

I would like to make a donation to support BRF Ministries.
Please use my gift for:

☐ Where it is most needed ☐ Anna Chaplaincy ☐ Living Faith

☐ Messy Church ☐ Parenting for Faith

Title	First name/initials	Surname	
Address			
			Postcode
Email			
Telephone			
Signature			Date

Our ministry is only possible because of the generous support of individuals, churches, trusts and gifts in wills.

Please treat as Gift Aid donations all qualifying gifts of money made (*tick all that apply*)

giftaid it

☐ today, ☐ in the past four years, ☐ and in the future.

I am a UK taxpayer and understand that if I pay less Income Tax and/or Capital Gains Tax in the current tax year than the amount of Gift Aid claimed on all my donations, it is my responsibility to pay any difference.

☐ My donation does not qualify for Gift Aid.

Please notify BRF Ministries if you want to cancel this Gift Aid declaration, change your name or home address, or no longer pay sufficient tax on your income and/or capital gains.

You can also give online at **brf.org.uk/donate**, which reduces our administration costs, making your donation go further.

Please complete other side of form ●

SHARING OUR VISION – MAKING A GIFT

Please accept my gift of:

☐ £2 ☐ £5 ☐ £10 ☐ £20 Other £ [ ]

by (*delete as appropriate*):

☐ Cheque/Charity Voucher payable to 'BRF'

☐ MasterCard/Visa/Debit card/Charity card

Name on card

Card no. [ ][ ][ ][ ] [ ][ ][ ][ ] [ ][ ][ ][ ] [ ][ ][ ][ ]

Expires end [M][M] [Y][Y] Security code* [ ][ ][ ]   *Last 3 digits on the reverse of the card

Signature   Date

☐ I would like to leave a gift to BRF Ministries in my will.
Please send me further information.

☐ I would like to find out about giving a regular gift to BRF Ministries.

For help or advice regarding making a gift, please contact
our fundraising team +44 (0)1235 462305

Your privacy

We will use your personal data to process this transaction.
From time to time we may send you information about
the work of BRF Ministries that we think may be of
interest to you. Our privacy policy is available at
brf.org.uk/privacy. Please contact us if you wish to
discuss your mailing preferences.

Registered with

FUNDRAISING
REGULATOR

◗ Please complete other side of form

Please return this form to 'Freepost BRF'
No other address information or stamp is needed

Bible Reading Fellowship is a charity (233280) and company limited by guarantee (301324),
registered in England and Wales

GL0324

Guidelines forthcoming issue

We hope you will join us for the next issue of *Guidelines*, which contains – as always – interesting themes and rigorous Bible analysis.

We continue our study of Luke alongside Loveday Alexander. Taking us through from the end of Jesus' teaching ministry in Galilee to the resurrection, Loveday helps us to see the cost of the path of peace that Jesus must tread. Max Kramer also travels with us on our journey through Lent with his notes on dealing with difficulty: how can the sufferings we observe in the Bible help shape how we understand the relationship between suffering and God, others, and ourselves? Meanwhile, Sharon Prentis helps us to see the joy of living for Christ in her notes on Philippians.

In the Old Testament, we will study Leviticus, a book which many of us may regard with either dread or indifference! Peter Hatton helps us through this difficult book to see its countercultural encouragement towards holiness. Walter Moberly helps us to read and understand Nehemiah, which takes place at a time when those who followed God felt decentralised and irrelevant – a timely parallel to post-Christendom today. Following our series on New Testament prayers in the previous issue, Valerie Hobbs will take us through a series on Old Testament prayers, helping us to resist the dominant culture of neoliberalism and pray in a way that honours God rather than ourselves.

Two further timely sets of notes encourage us to think about relevant issues. Andrew Smith's notes on multifaith engagement help us to position ourselves in a world where the numbers of those following other faiths are rising much faster than Christianity. How do we engage with people of other faiths with integrity and respect? Victoria Omotoso looks at the important topic of faith and culture, taking seriously Jesus' prayer in John 17 for unity alongside holiness.

Finally, David Spriggs gives us a fascinating series on Christian giving, while Siobhán Jolley brings us a new perspective on the much-maligned character of Mary Magdalene.

As ever, all of our contributors aim to bring you closer to the person and love of God.

What the Bible means to me: Isabelle Hamley

What the Bible means to me is a really personal question, linked to my entire journey as a Christian. I grew up in France, in a very secular environment, with parents who not only did not believe, but actively fought against religion in all its forms. But I always believed and always prayed. My family life was difficult and often violent, and praying to this unknown God was all I could do at times. But it was very much an unknown God. In secular France, there was nowhere for me to really explore or ask questions.

When I went to secondary school, I met a girl who walked the same way I did, and we became friends. Her dad had planted a church in the street next to mine, meeting in their home. Encouraged by her parents, she gave me a Bible to read and wisely told me not to start at the beginning! As I read the New Testament, I felt a sense of coming home: the God I had been praying to was here, in the pages of scripture. God finally had a name.

Two passages became defining moments: reading them got me to a point of faith and making a decision to follow the God who had reached out to me from early childhood. The first was Romans 8:38–39 (NRSV): '[Nothing] will be able to separate us from the love of God in Christ Jesus our Lord.' Growing up in a home where there was never enough love to go round, the promise of God's unshakeable love was a complete revelation, and a promise I have held on to for the whole of my life as a Christian. The second passage that brought me to God was 'perfect love casts out fear' (1 John 4:18, NRSV). Again, growing up with fear as a constant companion – fear of violence, rejection, failure, never being good enough – I was met with God's response to my deepest longing.

Becoming a Christian didn't change everything. Home remained a difficult place. Often, my only connection to God and church was through the pages of scripture: I read the Bible because it was my place of encounter with God, and hearing God speak. And this hasn't really changed. Today I still feel that I hear God most clearly through the pages of scripture. I read the Bible and, most often, I find something new, something deep, something challenging or comforting. I have friends who encounter God first through worship, in prayer, through other Christians. I do too, to a degree. But scripture always has been my best friend, my guide and my first way to conversation with God – 'a lamp to my feet and a light to my path' (Psalm 119:105, NRSV).

Recommended reading

God became flesh at Christmas. But how does God, who created all things, live within the limitations of humanity – limitations that humanity itself often resents and tries to transcend? And what does it truly mean to be human? As contemporary society grapples with questions of identity, justice and medical ethics, *Embracing Humanity* deftly explores how different aspects of being human are both inhabited and transformed in the incarnation.

Through the lens of Advent and Christmas, Isabelle Hamley guides us through daily reflections and prayers, encouraging us to meditate on being human in the light of God's choice to reach out to us in Jesus.

The following is an edited extract taken from the Introduction.

I grew up in a world without Christmas.

As a child in a virulently atheist family, going through the highly secular French education system, I simply did not hear the story of Christmas until I was a teenager. Of course, we had a tree and presents, and as an avid reader I came across rumours of Christmas in books, but nothing concrete or explicit. Christmas was just a cultural artefact, a time to get presents and endure distant relatives. Magic and wonder waned as soon as I stopped believing in Father Christmas (no mention of 'Santa' in my family, that would have been far too religious).

Watching my first nativity, age twelve, was a revelation. The sheer wonder of it still gives me goosebumps: the hard journey, the promise of a star, the extraordinary baby unrecognised while an indifferent world goes by. I still love nativities. In particular, I love school nativities. They're a wonderful, chaotic, odd take on the Christmas story. Sometimes they are so chaotic it is actually difficult to recognise much of the Christmas story in there, in between unicorns, aliens and robots. I love them, because they tug on a familiar story – after all, even in the weirdest, most outlandish interpretations, you still have Mary, Joseph and Jesus, and the wonder of the birth. At the same time, they bring in so much else – all the strange, quirky aspects of our humanity, with joy and celebration that we can't always explain, and the occasional bun fight between ox and donkey. School nativities are a cacophony of humanity. And this is the world, the people God has come to walk with, in their habits and cultures and choices, even the questionable ones.

Even when the message passes by those gathered, focused as they are on taking pictures of their own little cherubs dressed in makeshift donkey costumes, nevertheless, in this echo of the story, there is something of God-with-us, still often unrecognised, but present nonetheless. There is still something of God coming into the reality of our lives, right in the midst of them, and taking shape in the particularities of where we are. Christmas points us to who God is, but it also points us towards what it means to be human and how God chooses to become one of us.

The 21st century is a strange time to be human. Today rumours are not of God-made-flesh, but of artificial intelligence, which may make many humans redundant. God became flesh, but human beings seem constantly eager to escape being flesh: we make disincarnated, disembodied 'intelligence', in our image. We try to flee our bodies in virtual reality, and modern medicine gives us ways to change the bodies we do not like or want and prolong life far beyond previously natural ends. What can the Christmas story tell us about who we are in this changing world? What does it mean for the Good News to be good news for the whole human person, rather than just minds or souls? Who are we called to be, as we walk with the God who walks with us?

To be a Christian is to believe that God, the creator of the universe, is beyond anything we can imagine or fathom. Yet it is also to believe that this God, who created us, stooped to earth and chose to become one of us. It is to believe that in God's eyes, our humanity is not something to transcend, but something to embrace.

This Advent, I invite you on a journey to explore humanity in the light of Jesus' coming. Each day, we will explore a different aspect of Jesus' humanity, of God's wholehearted embrace of the world he created. Humanity is not an easy thing to live with; we often struggle with our limitations, and the realities of a physical world we cannot ever fully control, and a human world of interactions that brings as much pain as it brings joy. And yet this is the existence that God chose and embraced. God brought salvation not by removing us from our humanity, but by entering it, and inviting us into a journey of transformation within it.

To order a copy of this book, please use the order form on page 151 or visit **brfonline.org.uk**

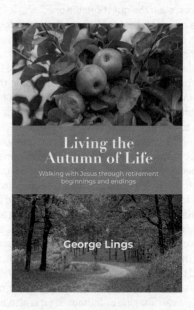

Living the
Autumn of Life

Walking with Jesus through retirement
beginnings and endings

George Lings

How can we best approach the season between retiring and becoming
dependent? Autumn is a time of gains and losses: fruit being harvested,
and leaves falling. This book charts the experience of living through
both realities, drawn from the author's own life and from the views of
interviewees. Informed by historic and contemporary reading, it offers
snapshots of later life, taken against a backdrop of ageism in society
and church. George Lings reflects on the identity of the 'active elderly',
and considers through a biblical lens the challenges and opportunities
that this season brings.

Living the Autumn of Life
Walking with Jesus through retirement beginnings and endings
George Lings
978 1 80039 282 3 £12.99
brfonline.org.uk

To order

Online: brfonline.org.uk
Telephone: +44 (0)1865 319700
Mon–Fri 9.30–17.00

Delivery times within the UK are normally 15 working days. Prices are correct at the time of going to press but may change without prior notice.

Title	Price	Qty	Total
BRF Advent Book: Embracing Humanity	£9.99		
A Calendar of Carols	£9.99		
Living the Autumn of Life	£12.99		

POSTAGE AND PACKING CHARGES			
Order value	UK	Europe	Rest of world
Under £7.00	£2.00	Available on request	Available on request
£7.00–£29.99	£3.00		
£30.00 and over	FREE		

Total value of books	
Donation*	
Postage and packing	
Total for this order	

* Please complete and return the Gift Aid declaration on page 143.

Please complete in BLOCK CAPITALS

Title .... First name/initials .... Surname ....

Address ....

.... Postcode ....

Acc. No. .... Telephone ....

Email ....

Method of payment

❑ Cheque (made payable to BRF) ❑ MasterCard / Visa

Card no. ☐☐☐☐ ☐☐☐☐ ☐☐☐☐ ☐☐☐☐ ☐☐☐☐ ☐☐☐☐

Expires end ☐M☐M ☐Y☐Y Security code* ☐☐☐ * Last 3 digits on the reverse of the card

We will use your personal data to process this order. From time to time we may send you information about the work of BRF Ministries. Please contact us if you wish to discuss your mailing preferences. brf.org.uk/privacy

Please return this form to:

BRF Ministries, 15 The Chambers, Vineyard, Abingdon OX14 3FE | enquiries@brf.org.uk
For terms and cancellation information, please visit brfonline.org.uk/terms.

Bible Reading Fellowship is a charity (233280) and company limited by guarantee (301324), registered in England and Wales

BRF Ministries needs you!

If you're one of our regular *Guidelines* readers, you will know all about the benefits and blessings of regular Bible study and the value of serious daily notes to guide, inform and challenge you.

Here are some recent comments from *Guidelines* readers:

'… very thoughtful and spiritually helpful. [These notes] are speaking to the church as it is today, and therefore to Christians like us who live in today's world.'

'You have assembled an amazingly diverse group of people and their contributions are most certainly thoughtful.'

If you have similarly positive things to say about *Guidelines*, would you be willing to share your experience with others? Could you ask for a brief slot during church notices or write a short piece for your church magazine or website? Do you belong to groups, formal or informal, academic or professional, where you could share your experience of using *Guidelines* and encourage others to try them?

It doesn't need to be complicated: just answering these three questions in what you say or write will get your message across:

- How do *Guidelines* Bible study notes help you grow in knowledge and faith?
- Where, when and how do you use them?
- What would you say to people who haven't yet tried them?

We can supply further information if you need it and would love to hear about it if you do give a talk or write an article.

For more information:

- Email **enquiries@brf.org.uk**
- Telephone BRF Ministries on **+44 (0)1865 319700** Mon–Fri 9.30–17.00
- Write to us at BRF Ministries, 15 The Chambers, Vineyard, Abingdon OX14 3FE

BRF
Ministries

Inspiring people of all ages to grow in Christian faith

At BRF Ministries, we long for people of all ages to grow in faith and understanding of the Bible. That's what all our work as a charity is about.

- Our **Living Faith** range of resources helps Christians go deeper in their understanding of scripture, in prayer and in their walk with God. Our conferences and events bring people together to share this journey, while our Holy Habits resources help whole congregations grow together as disciples of Jesus, living out and sharing their faith.

- We also want to make it easier for local churches to engage effectively in ministry and mission – by helping them bring new families into a growing relationship with God through **Messy Church** or by supporting churches as they nurture the spiritual life of older people through **Anna Chaplaincy**.

- Our **Parenting for Faith** team coaches parents and others to raise God-connected children and teens, and enables churches to fully support them.

Do you share our vision?

Though a significant proportion of BRF Ministries' funding is generated through our charitable activities, we are dependent on the generous support of individuals, churches and charitable trusts.

If you share our vision, would you help us to enable even more people of all ages to grow in faith? Your prayers and financial support are vital for the work that we do. You could:

- Support BRF Ministries with a regular donation;
- Support us with a one-off gift;
- Consider leaving a gift to BRF Ministries in your will (see page 154);
- Encourage your church to support BRF Ministries as part of your church's giving to home mission – perhaps focusing on a specific ministry;
- Most important of all, support BRF Ministries with your prayers.

Donate at **brf.org.uk/donate** or use the form on pages 143–44.

Bearing fruit

'Remain in me, as I also remain in you. No branch can bear fruit by itself; it must remain in the vine. Neither can you bear fruit unless you remain in me.'

JOHN 15:4 (NIV)

As a charity, BRF Ministries is always doing a huge assortment of things, from our Anna Chaplaincy team equipping people to minister to older people to our Messy Church team bringing Jesus to families across the world. From our Parenting for Faith ministry reaching parents and church leaders to transform ideas about how to raise God-connected children to our Living Faith resources that span so many different topics to help people to develop their faith journey.

At a glance these activities might seem distant or disparate but a closer look shows the vine from which all our ministries grow. The mission set out by Leslie Mannering over 100 years ago to which we still hold today: inspiring people of all ages to grow in faith. God is at the heart of all that we do and we are hugely thankful for all the fruits we have born through this work over the last century and more.

We want to keep building on this work, adapting, growing and finding even more glorious ways for people to grow in their faith while still remaining rooted to our mission.

This work would not be possible without kind donations from individuals, charitable trusts and gifts in wills. If you would like to support us now and in the future you can become a Friend of BRF Ministries by making a monthly gift of £2 a month or more – we thank you for your friendship.

Judith Moore
Fundraising development officer

Find out more at **brf.org.uk/donate** or get in touch with us on **01235 462305** or via **giving@brf.org.uk**.

> Give. Pray. Get involved.
> **brf.org.uk**

GUIDELINES SUBSCRIPTION RATES

Please note our new subscription rates, current until 30 April 2025:

Individual subscriptions
covering 3 issues for under 5 copies, payable in advance
(including postage & packing):

	UK	Europe	Rest of world
Guidelines 1-year subscription	£19.50	£26.85	£30.75
Guidelines 3-year subscription (9 issues)	£57.60	N/A	N/A

Group subscriptions
covering 3 issues for 5 copies or more, sent to one UK address (post free):

Guidelines 1-year subscription	£14.97 per set of 3 issues p.a.

Please note that the annual billing period for group subscriptions runs from 1 May to 30 April.

Overseas group subscription rates
Available on request. Please email enquiries@brf.org.uk.

Copies may also be obtained from Christian bookshops:

Guidelines	£4.99 per copy

> All our Bible reading notes can be ordered online
> by visiting **brfonline.org.uk/subscriptions**

All our Bible reading notes can be ordered online by visiting
brfonline.org.uk/subscriptions

Title _____ First name/initials _____ Surname _____

Address _____

_____ Postcode _____

Telephone _____ Email _____

Please send *Guidelines* beginning with the January 2025 / May 2025 /
September 2025 issue (*delete as appropriate*):

(*please tick box*)

		UK	Europe	Rest of world
Guidelines 1-year subscription	☐	£19.50	☐ £26.85	☐ £30.75
Guidelines 3-year subscription	☐	£57.60	N/A	N/A

Optional donation to support the work of BRF Ministries £ _____

Total enclosed £ _____ (cheques should be made payable to 'BRF')

Please complete and return the Gift Aid declaration on page 143 to make your
donation even more valuable to us.

Please charge my MasterCard / Visa with £ _____

Card no. ☐☐☐☐ ☐☐☐☐ ☐☐☐☐ ☐☐☐☐

Expires end ☐☐ ☐☐ Security code ☐☐☐ Last 3 digits on the reverse of the card

To set up a Direct Debit, please complete the Direct Debit instruction on page 159.

We will use your personal data to process this order. From time to time we may send you
information about the work of BRF Ministries. Please contact us if you wish to discuss your mailing
preferences **brf.org.uk/privacy**

Please return this form with the appropriate payment to:
BRF Ministries, 15 The Chambers, Vineyard, Abingdon OX14 3FE
For terms and cancellation information, please visit **brfonline.org.uk/terms**.

GUIDELINES GIFT SUBSCRIPTION FORM

☐ I would like to give a gift subscription (please provide both names and addresses):

Title .... First name/initials .... Surname ....

Address ....

.... Postcode ....

Telephone .... Email ....

Gift subscription name ....

Gift subscription address ....

.... Postcode ....

Gift message (20 words max. or include your own gift card):

....

....

Please send *Guidelines* beginning with the January 2025 / May 2025 / September 2025 issue *(delete as appropriate)*:

(please tick box)

	UK	Europe	Rest of world
Guidelines 1-year subscription	☐ £19.50	☐ £26.85	☐ £30.75
Guidelines 3-year subscription	☐ £57.60	N/A	N/A

Optional donation to support the work of BRF Ministries £ ....

Total enclosed £ .... (cheques should be made payable to 'BRF')

Please complete and return the Gift Aid declaration on page 143 to make your donation even more valuable to us.

Please charge my MasterCard / Visa with £ ....

Card no. ☐☐☐☐ ☐☐☐☐ ☐☐☐☐ ☐☐☐☐

Expires end ☐M☐M ☐Y☐Y Security code ☐☐☐ Last 3 digits on the reverse of the card

To set up a Direct Debit, please complete the Direct Debit instruction on page 159.

We will use your personal data to process this order. From time to time we may send you information about the work of BRF Ministries. Please contact us if you wish to discuss your mailing preferences **brf.org.uk/privacy**

Please return this form with the appropriate payment to:
BRF Ministries, 15 The Chambers, Vineyard, Abingdon OX14 3FE

For terms and cancellation information, please visit brfonline.org.uk/terms.

Bible Reading Fellowship is a charity (233280) and company limited by guarantee (301324), registered in England and Wales

You can pay for your annual subscription to our Bible reading notes using Direct Debit. You need only give your bank details once, and the payment is made automatically every year until you cancel it. If you would like to pay by Direct Debit, please use the form opposite, entering your BRF account number under 'Reference number'.

You are fully covered by the Direct Debit Guarantee:

The Direct Debit Guarantee

- This Guarantee is offered by all banks and building societies that accept instructions to pay Direct Debits.
- If there are any changes to the amount, date or frequency of your Direct Debit, Bible Reading Fellowship will notify you 10 working days in advance of your account being debited or as otherwise agreed. If you request Bible Reading Fellowship to collect a payment, confirmation of the amount and date will be given to you at the time of the request.
- If an error is made in the payment of your Direct Debit, by Bible Reading Fellowship or your bank or building society, you are entitled to a full and immediate refund of the amount paid from your bank or building society.
- If you receive a refund you are not entitled to, you must pay it back when Bible Reading Fellowship asks you to.
- You can cancel a Direct Debit at any time by simply contacting your bank or building society. Written confirmation may be required. Please also notify us.

Instruction to your bank or building society to pay by Direct Debit

Please fill in the whole form using a ballpoint pen and return with order form to:
BRF Ministries, 15 The Chambers, Vineyard, Abingdon OX14 3FE

Service User Number: | 5 | 5 | 8 | 2 | 2 | 9 |

Name and full postal address of your bank or building society

To: The Manager	Bank/Building Society
Address	
	Postcode

Name(s) of account holder(s)

Branch sort code

| | | – | | | – | | | |

Bank/Building Society account number

Reference number

Instruction to your Bank/Building Society
Please pay Bible Reading Fellowship Direct Debits from the account detailed
in this instruction, subject to the safeguards assured by the Direct Debit Guarantee.
I understand that this instruction may remain with Bible Reading Fellowship
and, if so, details will be passed electronically to my bank/building society.

Signature(s)

Banks and Building Societies may not accept Direct Debit instructions for some
types of account.

Ministries

Inspiring people of all ages to grow in Christian faith

BRF Ministries is the
home of Anna Chaplaincy,
Living Faith, Messy Church
and Parenting for Faith

As a charity, our work would not be possible without
fundraising and gifts in wills.
To find out more and to donate,
visit brf.org.uk/give or call +44 (0)1235 462305